DADDY THE 8TH

First published in 2016 by Reed Independent, Victoria, Australia.

Printed by Createspace.com, a division of Amazon.com.

Available as a printed book or an ebook from Createspace.com or
Amazon.com or Kindle estores, together with most major international online
outlets or bookshops with online ordering facilities:
paperback: ISBN 9780994531124
ebook: ISBN 9780994531131

Front cover: Dilani Priyangika Ranaweera, Dart Lanka Productions, Sri
Lanka

National Library of Australia Cataloguing-in-Publication entry:
Creator: Reed, Bill, author.
Title: Daddy the 8th/ Bill Reed
Edition: first
ISBN: 9780994531124 (paperback)
ISBN: 9780994531131 (ebook)
Notes: includes bibliographical reference.
Subjects: Drama/indigenous/black comedy
Dewey Number: A822.3

the play

DADDY THE 8TH

Bill Reed

R

As its earlier iteration titled 'Real Riot', this play got a 'listed-for-consideration' by the Sydney Theatre Company in 2004.

It has also been selected and listed by the Australia Script Centre on its website Australianplays.org.

The Backgrounds

November 4, 1982. Moree, New South Wales
Ronald 'Cheeky' McIntosh, only 19 years of age, Aborigine,
was shot dead during a clash between blacks and whites of
Moree. Warren Rocky Tighe and Stephanie Duke (a 17-year-
old girl), both indigenous people as well, were also shot and
seriously wounded.

These young unarmed people were pot-shotted at while they
emerged from their makeshift barricade, at the end of a dead-
end called Endeavour Lane following a pub brawl, started in
the Ned Kelly bar of the main-street Imperial Hotel. At about
1.30 am Friday, 'Cheeky' McIntosh and Tighe and Duke were
shot. When news of Cheeky's death came out, a full scale
street riot began and last until the Imperial's publican came out
blasting with his shotgun. The local police also used shotguns
to herd the protesting black community members near the
Mission; they arrested 17 of them for so-called drunken
behaviour. More than 1200 indigenous mourners were at
Cheeky's funeral a week later.

At the ensuing trial in Sydney's Central Criminal Court a year
later, three white men were found not guilty of murder and not
guilty of malicious wounding with the intention of causing
grievous bodily harm. Instead they were given 14-year
sentence on the lesser charges of manslaughter and maliciously
wounding. The Darlinghurst court erupted in anger when the
verdicts were read out.

Myall Creek Massacre 1838
The Myall Creek massacre near Gwydir River, in the central
New South Wales district of Namoi, involved the killing of up
to 30 unarmed Indigenous Australians by ten white Europeans
and one black African on 10 June 1838 at the Myall Creek near
Bingara in northern New South Wales. The events that
happened there are well-known but still remain outrageous.

1

The Setting

The setting is outdoors at a reconstructed barricade in
Endeavour Lane. This is not a full barricade, but rather of the
makeshift junk-rubbish that the victim Ronald Cheeky
McIntosh and his fellow Aboriginal mostly-youths could
frantically scrounge around and find in the dark of that night...
bits of wood, a tree branch of two, domestic junk.

Endeavour Lane was then a rubbish-filled dead-end running
between the local primary school and the old town tennis
courts -- wheel-track, sour-sob and bull-ant country. Only
schoolkids and those who have to pee – the pubs are just along
the road – keep the weeds from choking it.

The Characters

DADDY THE 8TH is conceived as having a substantial indigenous cast but, in that, it is flexible.

DADDY

70-year-old elder of the then Moree Mission. Always had the x-marks-the-spot painted on him. A hard and minority-lived life lived. He is not bitter, only sad; is not vengeful only instantly forgiving. He tries with all his might to live up to being an Elder but probably not even he believes it anymore.

HAMMER

the writer/director. The local Artificial Inseminator ('The Moree Bull') who goes around injecting local cows with pedigree bulls' semen – a profession perhaps explaining a sort of innate manipulator in him. A tragedian tragic. A cynic with a salesman's grittiness. A lower-deck lawyer. Has been up to his shoulders the proverbial so much he no longer knows the ins and outs. Has always pulled bits of paper out from one or other of his pockets.

HORRIE

Hammer's driver around the district for his AI rounds. If life was a costume drama he'd always be cast as the Black Plague. An impulsive butter-in. Watching his boss being up to his shoulder in cows' bums has given him a world view that a never-cowed overbearing attitude gets you ahead. If he ever was in a real riot, he'd be the last one standing… further back.

BIG BELLE

The indigenous community's midwife and general community Carer. Poker is her game. She'll punch your lights out, but smother you in kindness until your lights come on again. She is the midwife in any community she is in. Has been up to her shoulders in more woman than

HAMMER has in cows, and it shows. Independent; her mob has always stayed in camp when the others have upped and gone walkabout.

ORPH

The town's undertaker's assistant. Grooming bodies is her self-given task in life and this reflects in her bright-but-prissy manner. Like her chosen profession, her chosen conversation is always out of kilter. She is a walking show-stopper used to listeners on her slab not responding to her nonsequiturs. On her slabs, she has seen how the inevitable is so glum and full of full stops.

McINTOSH

22-year-old not-so-long-ago local cricketing hero, due for great things and carrying the local indigenous hopes on his shoulders, but who has fallen from grace by being thrown out of a representative training camp caught possessing. Now the community's big Let-Down. As a result, he is now realising his one sure thing left in life is getting 'laid into'. Like the real riot victim Cheeky McIntosh, he would walk away from the barricade when he decides enough's enough but others will always have other ideas about that. Will end up with more invisible scars than visible ones – and that's saying a lot.

Act I

(Propped on the barricade in a casual, disrespectful way is HORRIE. He is wielding a bit of the makeshift barricade's wood as a cricket bat.

He jumps down, draws a crease with his foot, takes guard on middle stump and yells back down lane:)

HORRIE: Okay, China, let's see what you got.

(He pretends a cricket ball comes hurtling down… it does come with a sound effect from CHINA, who is controlling sound at the top of the lane. He hooks it for, of course, a six.

HAMMER strolls in)

HAMMER: And you are doing what?

HORRIE: Think of me as the snot-nosed kids. One week after the riot, you're passing here, so you keep saying, and it's me not the school horrors you see using the barricade as a wicket.

HAMMER: And I'll keep saying it. They called it the Great Moree Race Riot. But you come past a week later. Nobody's bothered to even take the barricade down. Kids are having a hit on it.

HORRIE: Hey, is that real live history or what?

(HAMMER inspects the barricade and surrounds)

HAMMER: Not bad.

HORRIE: I did my best, boss.

(Finally, when no one else is fronting up…)

7

HORRIE: Wanna get started with the mood thing?

HAMMER: Why not?

> *(HORRIE puts 'bat' over his shoulder, puts his hand out for a piece of paper from HAMMER, receives it and steps forward as on a stage)*

HORRIE: Once in a far-off Aboriginal land…
> *(but stops for:)*
I got to thinking a bit last night…. like, bullets or lotsa shitty little flying pieces? What's this Winchester 30/30 anyway, rifle or shotgun?

HAMMER: Don't ask me.

HORRIE: You say you're going to write the thing.

HAMMER: That doesn't make me want to know what I'm talking about.
> *(indicates his cricket bat)*
It looks like you're making it cricket balls. That'll do.

> *(HORRIE nods 'well, that's okay too'. He mans up as though on stage again, reads from the paper-piece 'script':)*

HORRIE: (prologue-wise) Once upon a time in a far-off Aboriginal land the Elder challenged the great evil spirit Dhuramoolan. 'Dhuramoolan, you keep doing all these bad things to my people, but why don't you pop round tomorrer and do them to me instead.' The great evil spirit laughed: 'Rightio, Daddy, I'll be there sure as shoot'. So the great spirit turned up the next day, and the Elder said, 'Hey, you're early. Come back tomorrer and I'll be ready for you too right.' 'Today is tomorrer,' roared Dhuramoolan. 'No it ain't. Tomorrer's tomorrer,' the Elder said, 'You pop around tomorrer and take it all out on me, no sweat'. 'You're a real dingo of a blackfellah,

8

you know that?', roared Dhuramoolan again. But Dhuramoolan fronted up the next day, but got the same response come back tomorrer. That spirit fellah ended up having to go somewhere else to cause mischief.

(He waits for HAMMER's judgment. HAMMER merely shrugs not-bad. HAMMER finally sees the others are coming down the lane at last...)

HAMMER: *(at them)* Don't let anyone bust a boiler on my behalf.

(BIG BELLE and ORPH duly arrive without great enthusiasm)

HAMMER: (taking up business) Okay, if nobody's strained any sinews, let's pick out discussion from when the hail came through the roof last night.

BIG BELLE: You call that a hall?

HAMMER: It mightn't be the cricket club's changing rooms but it was called a hall a hundred years ago. Fire Trap Hall, ha ha. Each ticket comes with a fire blanket.

BIG BELLE: You could have given us more warning than this morning.

HAMMER: It's Sunday, who's busy?

ORPH: If it wasn't Sunday, I could have been working and not been able to make it.

(None can react to that)

HAMMER: I thought that instead of trying to get them to fix the roof, we could let the clouds roll in.

BIG BELLE: The clouds haven't rolled in for years.

9

ORPH: What about my allergies when they're at home?

HAMMER: All right, I overlooked about your allergies when I was picking my nose in the mirror. I apologise.

ORPH: And I suppose you didn't think about bringing the histamine.

HAMMER: (mock) Oh, bugger.

ORPH: I'll start wheezing.

HAMMER: But that's good! Wheeze away, Orph! Wheeze your lines. They expect us to wheeze. Marlon Brando made it okay with the wheezing, right?
   (*then*)
Where's our McIntosh? We can't start without our McIntosh.

BIG BELLE: How do we know where he is? You haven't even told us you've got one.

ORPH: Nice way to start off. The victim doesn't turn up.
   (*stops*)
You know that's never once happened to me?

HORRIE: You're the undertakers, chrissakes!

   (He gets a look of 'don't' from HAMMER)

HORRIE: Well… shissake.
   (*then, gripe*)
Look, I've already kicked it off.

BIG BELLE: Kicked what off?

   *(HORRIE doesn't know, only shrugs 'ask HAMMER'.
   Instead, he re-marks his guard at the 'crease', calls back
   up lane:)*

10

HORRIE: Do your worse, China!

(While he playacts a ball – with sound effects from CHINA down the way -- being bowled at him…)

BIG BELLE: You get us down here to play silly-buggers? I could be in church doing that. And what's China doing up the end of the lane there?

HORRIE: Some insurance company's promo tent he's commandeered. You know what a Hitler he gets like around a sound system.

BIG BELLE: After I just had twins and then triplets in the middle of the night, he should know what's a sound system.

ORPH: Excuse me… if we take things slowing down to almost dead still… then China would be where the bullet started… well, the nastiest-of-the-lot bullet at any rate… and we are approximately where that nastiest-of-the-lot bullet entered young Cheeky McIntosh between the third and fourth ribs, left lateral… that, even as we speak, we slowed down that nastiest-of-the-lot bullet to almost dead still, then that awful spectre of a projectile has now moved something like eight metres out of the… mind you , this is only a guestimate… near-enough-to 150 metres it has to travel to here. Meaning poor young Cheeky McIntosh has theoretically only 142 metres to live… or to put it another way, near enough to one-seventh of a kilometre from becoming a victim and central to our entry into the drama festival. Isn't that awful?

HAMMER: Haven't you had coffee yet?

ORPH: No.

HAMMER: ('that explains it') Maybe we can get our minds off of entry wounds. You're not at work now. It's Sunday, remember.

11

ORPH: (high horse) I just think you can't bring things outside and not face up to equations that cannot be envisaged inside. That makes the air conditioning stop working, no two ways about it. I've had so many Sundays ruined like that, you know.

(They are obviously used to being long-suffering about her)

BIG BELLE: Look, Orph, we're sorry, okay.

ORPH: (still offended) I was only talking of a speeding bullet I feel exposed to out here in the open that might be a speeding bullet standing still but it's still a speeding bullet travelling at someone's speed of sound, nearly.

HORRIE: (eagerness easily lost) That'd be China's.

ORPH: What?

HORRIE: China's speed of sound.

(He tails off since he's not really interested)

BIG BELLE: (at HAMMER) Couldn't you find a horror wax works or something it would have been nicer to front up in?

ORPH: (can't help herself) A speeding bullet is straight-forward thing. I've seen the results. It spins in the air on its trajectory. Bullets have Fate like us too, you know.

(HAMMER rounds on BIG BELLE)

HAMMER: I asked you to meet up with him.

BIG BELLE: Who?

HAMMER: Our Cheeky McIntosh.

BIG BELLE: Look, sport, I've been pulling cheeky little buggers out of women all night. Don't push it.

HAMMER: Well, you could have said.

BIG BELLE: I've been following umbilicals, now I want to follow running a bath.

> *(She steps back into some dog's dropping; blames HAMMER of course)*

BIG BELLE: Shit!

HAMMER: That's what I mean! That's what we're down here to check out. The dog's shit beneath our wings!

BIG BELLE: You could have at least paid a bit extra to get the place shot of the dog's crap.

HAMMER: What to do? It's a public lane. Dogs've spilled their hot dinners down here for dog generations. Dogs have their sacred sites too.
> *(calling up to end of lane about annoying static in air)*
What's with the static, China?
> *(makes throat-cutting kill-it motion)*
Buzzing. Worse than whispering, buzzing. Buzzing, buzzing, it gives me the creeps. At least in Redfern you can't hear the flies buzzing over the traffic. Oh, give me the traffic!

BIG BELLE: It ain't buzzing. It's dog shit and I've stepped into it twice.

HORRIE: (suddenly butting in) I say it's ptochocracy!

HAMMER: ('not again') Please… it's Sunday morning.

HORRIE: Get this: I read where we're allowing all our sorry lives to be governed by beggars… any coloured beggars, not just white beggars, so nobody gets offended. That's the trouble

with us lot. Ptochocratically speaking. This country; Moree
here.
   (sweeps hand indicating all beyond)
Well, it's up to us, that's what.

HAMMER: And that is?

HORRIE: Ptochocracy. Jeez, nobody listens to a bloke.

BIG BELLE: Why are we waiting anyway? Forget whoever
you've got for Cheeky McIntosh.

HAMMER: (enthusiastically) I managed to get Cheeky
McIntosh to play him. He's the real Cheeky's nephew cousin
or something, spitting image – or was, if you want to nitpick,
ha ha.
   (then)
Horrie's already kicked off. Orph, you're up second.

ORPH: What for?

HAMMER: The mood, the mood.

BIG BELLE: If you've finally got someone for Cheeky
McIntosh, does the Actors Guild of Australia have to get it in
triplicate first or something? Why the suspense? What are we
kicking our heels down this shitty place anyway?

HAMMER: That's the mood! Go on!

ORPH: ('it's my turn, not yours') Excuse me. One thing you
learn from the slab is lines are not all that lines seem to be.
You look down a line of sight and what do you mostly find?
You find a bee line, that's what.

HAMMER: ('now my turn') Absolutely! Look, you're
standing on a Nullarbor outcropping on your head and in the
sky what do you see but none other than the Great Serpent
making ways and means for us all. So now all we have to

decide is: are the tribes gathering in one spot or are we too busy looking up at the sky standing on our heads with spear and bull-roarer on a Nullarbor outcrop to know that? That's the to be or not to be of our wanting to be actors.

ORPH: Not if it means standing on my head in the Nullarbor. Not while my poor Dad's waiting back home for his medicine.

HAMMER: (kneels to pat earth) Call this piece of Moree the bare boards of our stage back at the hall. We mightn't be able to see through it like our stage back at the hall, but we know you are down there young Cheeky McIntosh, you pesky teenager of an indigene, you. We wait for you, as we wait at this place of foul murder of your innocence. Come on, Cheeky, come out. It's the Moree riot of 1982 and it's getting impatient.

HORRIE: (singsong) Cheeky, come!

BIG BELLE and ORPH: Come, Cheeky!

ALL: (orchestrated by HAMMER) Come, Cheeky, come!

> *(Their attention, though, is taken by the sky darkening. Immediately, there comes from up the top of the lane a 'headlight' beam which keeps dipping from low to high beam and vice versa. Shortly after comes the threatening revving of cars.*
>
> *They all shield their eyes, temporarily blinded. Only HORRIE is brave enough to stand up to the beam; he playacts taking guard on middle stump and facing up to it:)*

HORRIE: Send down all you've got, China!

> *(There is the whirring of a cricket ball which, blinded, HORRIE can only hope he swings in proximity to. It hits him in the crutch. He doubles up in pain.*

*At least this stops the headlights and the darkening of
the sky.*

They are able to adjust to the natural sunlight again.

*When they do, the women and HORRIE are stunned to
see DADDY lying on the ground by the barricade, flat
out on his back. They turn to HAMMER for an
explanation but HAMMER has not noticed any of this.
He is too busy being peevish about the intruding
headlights and gesturing smarten-up towards the end of
the lane where CHINA is.*

*DADDY finally wearily rises and hoists his overnight
bag to shuffle off. He passes HAMMER blatantly close,
but without breaking the latter's concentration on the
end of the lane)*

DADDY (muttering as he goes) I said stop buggerisin' around
an' go home, y'silly buggers.

*(Except HAMMER, they stare open-mouthed after him.
BIG BELLE has to go over to tap HAMMER on the
shoulder)*

BIG BELLE: Hey, master blacktracker, who was that?

HAMMER: Who was who? Or whom. Whom was who or
whom was who, mmm?

BIG BELLE: Shut up. Who've you roped in without telling
us?

HAMMER: Who me?

BIG BELLE: You.

HAMMER: (seeing no one else) Who?

16

BIG BELLE: (furiously, after DADDY) Him!

HORRIE: (backing her up) That old guy.

(HAMMER stares at them open-mouthedly. When DADDY comes back as a nearing shadow, BIG BELLE physically cranes his head around to see DADDY)

HAMMER: Oh, *him*? So what?

BIG BELLE: Don't play dumb.

HAMMER: It's a free country. I'm allowed to.

BIG BELLE: I mean him, *here*.

HAMMER: Let's put it this way: did he look, you know, real old?

ORPH: Let me put it this way, I wouldn't have let him sit up and just walk off one of my slabs at work, no I wouldn've. I'd be working on the premise that, if he was on one of my clients, he wouldn't be capable of sitting up and sliding off my slab, I know.

HAMMER: Say, old, like before or after the coffin stage?

BIG BELLE: You just answer the question.

HAMMER: I don't know how to. I never saw his face.

ORPH: You see this is what can happen if you leave them lying out in the sun with the crows and the cockies, and I'm not talking cockies with the head feathers, I'm talking cockroaches. The worst is they go for the rims of the eyes and the lips first. I keep telling my own old Dad that. At least he takes a blind bit of notice.

HAMMER: Are we saying here that we had an apparition? Horrie?

(HORRIE can only surlily shrug)

HAMMER: I'm going to take that as a yes. Did we have a visit from an apparition of our Daddy? So, where's our apparition going, having come?

BIG BELLE: For Christ's sake, what Daddy?

HAMMER: My cast list's Daddy!

BIG BELLE: You haven't put a word down yet.

HAMMER: I have! I can't help it if I write so badly my keyboard won't cooperate.

BIG BELLE: We're supposed to be into a rehearsal by now.

HAMMER: That's why we're out here for this morning.

BIG BELLE: *Why?*

HAMMER: To see what gives, what else? For the jottings-down of the look-see and their authentics. You're the one who said it… for the Ghosts That Are Appearin'.

HORRIE: (echo silliness) Where be Daddy? Who be Daddy?

HAMMER: That's right! Figment or who cares a fig, ladies! Where be our Daddy? Give it up, Horrie!

(quickly hands him another piece of paper)

HORRIE: There was a little man and no man who had a little gun and no gun who saw a little old Daddy and no little old Daddy and shot him and did not shoot him dead and not dead with his Winchester 30/30 and no Winchester 30/30!

18

HAMMER: (taking it up, into air) Oh, Daddy! Oh, Mein Papa! Oh, me oh my! Please emerge from the mange of the vintage Moree of the Eighties. Come on, Dads! What more do you want? The old ways? The old frays? Sure, why not? Aren't you the headman around here? Don't they call you the Man on the Mission ha ha? All right, we'll make you the Noble Savage. Loin cloth to your cods, you've got it. Spear and spear-thrower, say no more! Mud make-up and peering into the Dreaming horizon?, sure, no probs!
    (and)
Roll up, roll up, and see the noblest Daddy of them all back on the killing field of Endeavour Lane on a dark and chilly chilling and bitter Moree November night!

HORRIE: Come on, Dads, for fuck's sake.

BIG BELLE: (disgusted with them) He was flat out to it by that...
    (meaning barricade)
contraption there. That's what you two should be, too.

HAMMER: (knocks on barricade) Moree. Here. I make it so. Moree-upon-Mehi. Nice ring to it, that. I dub thee Moree of the Southern Cistern Seas.

BIG BELLE: That was no figment, was it, Orph?

ORPH: It was not or who knows away from the slab? Or not.

HAMMER: I was using the Divine Abstract.

BIG BELLE: (eyes heavenward) Good God.

HAMMER: (theatrical flourish) I will ignore that by pointing out that if mere prop-men, using a few screwdrivers, are able to string a few bits of wood together and say, right, this 'ere be a barricade, the site of some national shame... no, more... that this 'ere be the specific lane between school, tar-crusted tennis courts and flood channel at back, a locale where butchery thrives as much as it lingers… well, by my light, I claim that to add: Daddy is alive and well in the delusions of our minds before coffee on a Sunday morning. That's all. Over and out.

BIG BELLE: Big one hand clapping, sport.

(In the silence that follows:)

HORRIE: See how you go, China!

(Shapes up to another ball coming whizzing. He tries a cover drive, is obviously bowled comprehensively.

HAMMER rummages in his pocket for another piece of paper)

HAMMER: I say again.
   (reads from paper)
This is our tribal land of the once'n'noble Moree mob, descendants of the famed Kamilroi tribe of old, out of the gene pool of which Daddy, mythical hero of our play-waiting-in-the-wings, hurriedly visits around midnight, on a Thursday-stroke-Friday night in November 1982, the dozen or so of our hair-brained youths barricaded down the bottom of the lane called Endeavour after the bottles and billiard balls had started flying. I take a breath.
   (then)
Dads to the rescue.
   (stands, dusts himself down)
Neither of you may have realise it, but I have just retrieved your sense of stage reality. You needn't thank me. It's perfectly free.
   (shouts out into air)
Take breaks and don't forget I take mine milk and two sugars.

BIG BELLE: We're taking more than a break.
   (indicates after DADDY)
After who's just turned up, we just might go on strike, sport.

(And makes to go off, but he stops her with not a little desperation.)

HAMMER: No, seriously. Imagine if Daddy was a real person right now. Imagine him, thirty-five years to the day, for the sake of what we're doing here in the first place...
'Tis now the very witching time of night
When the empties gape and hot fumes are breathed out'...
Imagine him stumbling arthritically out of the old Mission house about a mile up that way. The word has gone around about the riot down at the Imperial. His old tribal heart is heartedly sick of it all. He has an old pair of cut-away strides tied around his waist and a soiled flannel banyan, whatever that is. He is the Daddy the Elder to the rescue. No shoes. Craggy feet as hard as old leather. His old croc's eyes glisten past a lifetime of the fly-blown when he spots the smoke coming from Endeavour Lane, but he doesn't know it's Endeavour Lane yet. Already one word is on his lips. It is the guttural for all seasons – the 'Eh'. Out of all the swim it's now Daddy and the big 'Eh' Eh, eh? And so, from down here in Moree...
   (stomps on the ground)
Daddy, today's Kamilroi's answer to the cavalry coming over the hill. Daddy of the once-fiery Kamilroi shuffles thundering towards the smoke rising from Endeavour Lane just as surely as if he was up down the end of the real lane in real time but without the moonlight that made sighting down the barrel that night so easy.

(Disgustedly, BIG BELLE roughly turns his head around so that he can see DADDY backing in looking very confused about where he is, and finally deciding to sit down on a clump of grass on the tennis-court side.

BIG BELLE snaps her fingers in HAMMER's face and removes herself, leaving HAMMER – just as confused -- with the old man. He goes to step forward to DADDY, stops, steps back. He keeps repeating this. They finally settle into staring at each other mesmerically)

21

ORPH: As we speak… and I don't mind telling you… that speeding bullet near stood still has continued on its path and almost certainly has passed the 72nd metre mark of 150 metres. And everybody knows it goes faster on a Sunday morning. I'd speculate it's the clearer air.

BIG BELLE: Leave off, orright, Orph?

ORPH: I'm only trying to point out how nothing much moves on Sunday morning. Around Moree, it's usually bullets. The reason why I say that is at work we hardly ever get a deceased on Sunday mornings. So it's even the dead who are not moving. Or are.

HORRIE: You're not open on Sunday mornings, shissake!

ORPH: Now you know our trade secret.

(BIG BELLE hisses at HAMMER re DADDY)

BIG BELLE: Stop bashing him up with your eyes!

(Her interruption allows HAMMER makes bold enough to edge towards DADDY especially when the old man tears himself away to turn and try to find somewhere comfortable on the ground to sit)

DADDY: (mumble*)* Where the buggery…

(HAMMER jumps as though he has had a small electric shock when he hears DADDY actually speak. He does, though, turn away to then try to ignore DADDY's presence… whistles, squats, picks at the grass around the barricade, examines the slab of cardboard carton that has been used as a wicket, goes over to ORPH, forgets what he wanted to say and backs away from her too… and so forth, until he can stand it no longer. He whips around to DADDY.)

22

HAMMER: *You mind*?

DADDY: (startled*)* You sittin' here?

HAMMER: Never mind where I'm sitting!

DADDY: Real ripe of you.

> *(The old man sits back)*

BIG BELLE: *(*indicating DADDY*)* Explain that then, magic man.

> *(HAMMER refuses to answer. Surlily he removes himself to the far side of the lane to think more about this.*
>
> *HORRIE saunters over to DADDY who now seems to be napping. He examines the old man, enjoying it all. He prods DADDY with his foot.)*

DADDY: *(*responding into air) I'm comin'! Don't go doin' anything mad, you blokes!

> *(and coughs throatily at the exertion. It has also made HORRIE jump back too. As a cover-up to that, he returns to in front of the barricade, marks his guard)*

HAMMER: *(*had enough*)* You! Old man!

> *(But for the moment DADDY is dead to the world -- and, anyway, YOUNG McINTOSH arrives. He has cuts and bruises to his face. When they see him, the women flock to him in commiseration)*

HAMMER: You're late.

BIG BELLE: Oh, yeah, don't ask him about his cuts and bruises.

HAMMER: Oo, look, you're all cut and bruised. You're late.

McINTOSH: Had a real stiff trot.

HAMMER: There are no stiff trots when it comes to assembly for ensemble work… 'assembly for ensemble work', not bad… unless someone…
  (*daggers at DADDY*)
drags them in from outside.

McINTOSH: I got real lost.

BIG BELLE: Well, you've come to the right place, love.

McINTOSH: Just that I shot over to Newcastle, see a few mates and got dragged off the street to make up this 'ere all-black line-up they had. I was standing there in that line looking real innocent and suddenly they hauled me out and laid into me for looking like a Muslim trying to infiltrate one of their black line-ups. We're particular about out all-black line-ups they said. I said you coulda fooled me and, like, I ain't Muslim anyway, and they laid into me for being a lying bloody Muslim, they said. So I lied and said okay I'm a Muslim and they laid into me again for being cheeky.

HAMMER: You are Cheeky.

McINTOSH: I tried that one too. I said back in Moree I'm playing Cheeky McIntosh in a real theatre play. He used to be me cousin and nobody's yet laid into me for *that,* so if you don't mind I'll kick off back to Moree I said. But they laid into me for lying about being a black fellah and then for being a rellie of a troublemaker they said, and then they laid into me for coming from Moree and then again for telling them I was from Moree when they hadn't asked and for presuming they wanted to know. Watch the nose, I said. Then they laid into

24

me again but now I'm forgetting what I'm being laid into for. I
don't know how many times they laid into me. They said they
wished they had me in a cell for a night. I said there's not
enough rope in China for me to hang around in a cell all night,
ha ha. Boy, did they lay into me for that. They're a hard mob
over in Newcastle.

HAMMER: Never mind, you're our very own Ronald Cheeky
McIntosh now, Macca. Up on the barricade with you. Watch
putting too much weight on it, but.

McINTOSH: I get a bit of a weapon? I got a bit of laying into
some other bugger to do m'self. A cricket bat like his'd do real
good. Maybe a few nails in it.

HAMMER: Er… no. This is going to be more on the peaceful
side of things.

McINTOSH: That right? What's the point?

BIG BELLE: (the midwife) McIntoshes from out Arunga
way?

McINTOSH: We're all from there long way back.

BIG BELLE: I reckon I hoicked you out of your mother.

HAMMER: Don't take any notice of how that rather large lady
expresses herself.

McINTOSH: Could do with a bit of shut-eye, but.

HAMMER: Exactly how the Cheeky you're playing feels!
You're dying to kip out but the white larries have driven you
lot down this lane and you're too het up. It's the blackfellahs'
dilemma, right? You can't open your eyes but you don't dare
shut them either. The hot blood and the stale piss is still
pumping through your veins but slowing. Here comes the start
of the hangover.

(McINTOSH 'uses' the barricade to ham the part)

McINTOSH: Yeah.

HAMMER: And, truth be known, down deep you're always knew it would come to this, right? Right, Cheeky McIntosh?

McINTOSH: Too right.

HAMMER: The trouble is you've been down here for maybe over an hour and there's only been a lot of shouting and honking from the whities up the lane. The buzz is starting to wear off a bit. Buzz, buzz. You maybe tell your mates Rocky Tighe and Stephie Duke, and the others, bugger this for a lark. Quick; before you can't help yourself dropping off, ask me 'what'.

McINTOSH: What?

> *(NOTE: as HAMMER describes it, spurred on by directorial hand movements from him, the others do their haphazard best to re-enact it. It is very sloppy and unenthusiastic)*

HAMMER: What, you ask? Shag almighty, the feeling of danger, that's what! Out there in the night, past your piss-weak attempt at a bonfire, up along the lane and over in the park over there... can't you ever hear them wolfing in this, the thickest part of this darkling!... well, scrub round that... yes, out there are 30 or so whitefellahs now... a few months ago, the same dudes you're your schoolmates, Cheeky... and now they're baying for your blood. They're over there under the trees in their pick-ups and old Holden bombs and they've got their banks of hunting spots on trained on down here and they've hands on their horns and their elastic-sideds on the accelerators and they're getting themselves riled up to actually do something about you. But they're not doing *anything*. Their revving engines, their drum roll, their calling cards. The

26

trouble is your eyelids are going and you're getting that stale grog thump-thump up top. Better call it a day and go crash out at home rather than waiting for a bunch of white pussies to make up their minds. Knock it off, you go. Cut it out, you white dickheads. Enough's enough. See you tomorrow round the back.

McINTOSH: (a bit spooked) It feels different once you get down here.

HAMMER: Of course it's different down here! All you've got between you and them is Rocky Tighe's broken billiard cue and a bit of…
   (*HORRIE waves his 'cricket bat'*)
pine box that the schoolkids next door used as a cricket bat, but regrettably you won't be around to know about that.

ORPH: Excuse I, there's no need to be so blunt about the dead. They don't just lie there; they squeak, you know.

> *(This is a real conversation stopper. Even, after a long pause, when HAMMER goes to carry on, BIG BELLE stops him for:)*

BIG BELLE: What're you on about, they squeak?

ORPH: Not everyone can hear it.

> *(ORPH offers nothing more, although they do wait just in case. Finally, HAMMER carries on:)*

HAMMER: Okay. So, Cheeky McIntosh… you're getting real shagged out. What's with these white buggers? You've grown up with most of them and you know how they're mostly all piss and wind when it comes down to it, right? Bang! Bang!, bang!, go their .22s and thump-thump go their roo double-barreled, but it's all up in the air, right?

HORRIE: (interjecting) And the Winchester 30/30.

HAMMER: And the old faithful 30/30. That's Leddingham and Delamothe and Wilmott. You know them, Cheeky. Old school chums, yep. You skun knees together. You lined up in the backs together. You head-high tackled together. But now old schoolmate Delamothe, he's got this cut on the head from you, trying to live down being seen dropping like a shaking log instead of getting in a few back on you. Leddingham and Wilmott take him home to get cleaned up. They pull his Dad's old 30/30 from the cupboard but by this time, way past the witching hour, Cheeky, you're tired, sure. You're bone weary. You figure you'll call time, beetle off home, sleep it all off.

McINTOSH: Stuff it, what's it been?

HAMMER: It's been more than two hours down here, if that's what you're asking.

McINTOSH: (nodding) Stuff it.

    (He starts dozing on the barricades)

HAMMER: Stuff it, yes sir. You and Rocky and your little sort, Stephie. The three of you snap your fingers; stuff it, let's choof! The fire's going. The barricades falling apart. The honking and the lights up in the park are dying down. You take your little sheila Stephie's hand and walk on back down the lane called Endeavour, one arm waving we're calling it a night. But...
    (pauses for effect)
who can forget about old faithful, the Winchester 30/30?

    (For a time, nobody moves.

    Then, HAMMER-allowed, HORRIE shouts 'hoi' back up lane to CHINA and gestures okay.

    They cup their ears as a signal for CHINA to 'sound out' a rifle crack. Nothing comes. HAMMER fills in:)

HAMMER: Back down the lane to reality. Even the mosquitoes whining in the night. No, as the night. As all of the night.

> *(Belatedly, there is a pretty feeble rifle report. At least it is enough to set HAMMER and HORRIE off again. HAMMER shoves another piece of paper in HORRIE's hand)*

HORRIE: (reading, declaiming) In such a night stood young Cheeky with a willow in 's hand upon the wild Mcree banks.

HAMMER: The old 30/30's slugs zinging over your head as you come back down the lane waving but that's only enough to make Leddingham and Delamothe and Wilmott crave to stop frigging around and really let fly at you. They lower their aim. Which one really and truly does so? Who really cares now? How can you have any idea with those headlights in your eyes? You'd thought they'd switch them off on your say-so. And then… and then…

> *(There is a type of frightened pause, posed theatrically by all, before McINTOSH breaks the mood:)*

McINTOSH: So can I hit the hay for a bit?

> *(This breaks the mood, much to HAMMER's disgust)*

HAMMER: Absolutely not.

BIG BELLE: You blaming him for something now?

HAMMER: Who, me?

McINTOSH: Where do you want me?

HAMMER: ('that's better') Take Rocky's broken billiard cue… well pretend for now you take Rocky's broken billiard cue… and you man and unman, a-man-ing and a-unman-ing go, one foot forwards, half a foot backwards, up the lane…

(At least McINTOSH is keen:)

McINTOSH: Yeah, and…?

(HAMMER is encouraged to get any sort of cooperation)

HAMMER: And… we improvise!
(to the others)
All… warm ups!

(But he himself can only start to run around in a circle. At almost the same time, BIG BELLE begins running up and down on the spot, as best she can.

HORRIE and ORPH take her lead. They too start running on the spot.

Not even this ludicrousness can last long. They wind down. McINTOSH fills the awkward, 'we're useless' silence:)

McINTOSH: (a stopper) Can I warm up with a bit of shut-eye?
(then meaning DADDY)
Who's that?

(Mention of DADDY has HAMMER stopping)

HAMMER: I see no one. I see only supposition. All I suppose is that any unwanted supposition is supposed to be Daddy but don't quote me.

McINTOSH: M'uncle Daddy once removed?

HAMMER: Don't stop at once, remove him again by all means.

McINTOSH: Thought I recognised him. M'Dad always said he was a bit of a Jackie.
  (*confidentially*)
Bit all-Koori n' up himself, like.

HAMMER: Well, that would be right, if he was Daddy, which I'm not saying he is.

BIG BELLE: Yeah, you wouldn't.

> *(In the silence, which is the only thing that could be a response to that, McINTOSH tries to climb onto the barricade, but it collapses beneath him. Again, there is nothing for anybody to do but accept the mounting chaos.*
>
> *Finally, the young man puts his head back over the barricade)*

McINTOSH: This, like, all you're paying me to do?

HAMMER: Maybe, maybe not.

McINTOSH: But no lines, right?

HORRIE: Didn't he say he was desperate to become an actor?

McINTOSH: I am. It's the lines, not me.

HAMMER: All you have to do is stand up there and take one for the team.

McINTOSH: One what?

HAMMER: (shrugging) A zing, a ping, a ffffluttt. You won't feel a thing.

31

McINTOSH: But no scars, right?

HAMMER: Hopefully you'll be the only one to make a lasting impression.

McINTOSH: I'm sick of being laid into.

(DADDY snaps awake)

DADDY: Eh?
  (but before anyone can answer)
Orphie said to get down here quicksmatt. Am I here, eh?

HAMMER: What here?

DADDY: Orphie. Seen her around? My daughter, eh? She borrowed a mate's ute to see a man off, then ups and ends up at the Imperial when I said no. Little sheilas today, eh? You from around here?
  (gets no answer)
Seventy-three if I'm a day, but be buggered if I won't see them whitefellah kids get away with starting the blue with our boys. You sick of it too?

> *(and closes his eyes again. HAMMER hurries over to look down the lane)*

HAMMER: *(calling to CHINA)* Who let him in, China?

HORRIE: (backing him up) No letting any more in, China. We're trying to work here.

BIG BELLE: You call this work?

HORRIE: If I'm on the clock, I'll call anything work.
  (at her size)

You put me on the clock, I'll even work around you. It'd have to be a minimum of a half day to get in one circle around you, but.

BIG BELLE: You trying to be funny?

HORRIE: If you're going to beat me up, no.

(BIG BELLE, by way of displacement, gets defensive to HAMMER about DADDY)

BIG BELLE: I found him at the urinal, if you must know.

HAMMER: In the Men's toilet up there?

BIG BELLE: *(defiantly)* So what?

HAMMER: Don't you have any idea who he's trying to impersonate?

BIG BELLE: Lay off. Bit of luck the poor old sport's brought his lawyer along.

HAMMER: (reverting to type) Two people. In the middle of the rush hour, they rush into each other's arms, make violent love against a traffic light, then move on zipping up. They have no idea who the other is. They only know that once a week for the last twenty years they have bumped into each other and rutted on that traffic light like two rabbits with congenital hives. That's what we've got here. Coincidence if you only pass that traffic light once at that time. More times than that, it's obsession.

ORPH: I agree with that. You try making them up to look like they did ten or twenty years ago. I was say to each one when I've finished up, 'Kindly don't come back again'. I mean, one's only trying to be nice ignoring their awful state of dead.

(She gets the usual confounded pause)

33

HAMMER: (calls) We been videoing all this, China?

(He gets a sound-effect click, which could mean anything, and also ORPH has had an inevitable second thought on the matter)

ORPH: However, regarding that sort of traffic light, personally I've had quite enough lifting legs without much result in my time.
  (indicates DADDY but accusing HAMMER)
And that ain't good taste.

BIG BELLE: You've said it, girl.

DADDY: *(*looking up*)* Y'see Orphie, tell her no probs, I'm down here, eh?

(They don't know how to answer that. Of course, BIG BELLE blames HAMMER)

BIG BELLE: You should have seen your slack gob when you saw him. Big magic man conjuror.

HAMMER: *(*carefully*)* Who said it's him?

BIG BELLE: I asked him. You squashed maggot.

HAMMER: (nonchalance*)* Maggot I might be, but I would still have a maggot's point of view. How can it be Daddy? You think about it. How's he going to turn up here now when it's debatable if he ever got around to turning up here back in '82? Alternatively, I might grant you that he lives...
  (stomping on ground)
all round here but, even then, you'd be choking coincidence. And I'd reckon choking more like a witchetty grub than a maggot. Better in the blender from my experience.

ORPH: (to DADDY) Old man like mine at home, you ever heard of Aboriginal Legal Aid?

HAMMER: Hey, nobody sueing anybody.
  (whisper)
He dropped off before he heard that?

BIG BELLE: No, he's just working up the energy to get at your jugular. And that's in your damn hip pocket.

HAMMER: *(decision)* My fellow tribals, are we or are we not wasting precious time? We should be following our suggestions, no?...
  (has to resort to HORRIE)
What do you suggest, Horrie?

HORRIE: Boss, I'd lay a bet you'd be suggesting we pull together.

HAMMER: Absol-bloody-utely! At this our first gathering in Endeavour Lane where even the great Australian sun shines down sadly...
  (at DADDY)
that, for a start, it would be a great help if you cleared off, old fritz.

  (Waits, but DADDY doesn't move)

BIG BELLE: We had no idea he even existed. You weren't even going to change his name, you back end.

HAMMER: Hey, what's special about any 'Daddy', even if he's any 'Daddy'? He taken out a copyright on the name? What I can't see in the attitudes I feel going around is why are we getting our DNA strands in a twist.

ORPH: ...other than the way they're twisted.

HAMMER: …other than the way they're twisted. Just assume that this is the real Daddy of the long line of Daddy elders. So what? It could be said we're working together to get his other Daddy up on the stage where it belongs. That's all I'm saying

HORRIE: … in a pulling-together kind of way.

HAMMER: … in a pulling together kind of way.

ORPH: … but not quite right, almost but not quite.

HAMMER: … but not quite right, almost but not quite.
  (*realizes what she is doing*)
Will you cut that out?

> (*but he too gets blank stares. He has to sail on now:*)

HAMMER: So, okay, granted. It's Daddy of the Moree mob, the proper Poppa. Dozing on a comfy corner of the theatrical garden called Endeavour Lane. So what?

BIG BELLE: (outraged) So what? I've had this. You couldn't put on the squirts.

> (*and she walks out on him*)

HAMMER: *(*after her*)* And you need a lifesaver to tug in the slack.

> (*She strides back on, grabs him by the shirt front.*)

HAMMER: Beat me. I'm suffering already.

> (*She releases him with disgust, angrily strides off down lane again*)

ORPH: This is precisely what I tell smokers who end up on my slab.

(She stops suddenly, doesn't elaborate. In any case, this coincides with BIG BELLE, equally without explanation, returning and:)

BIG BELLE: Tell them what?

ORPH: That there's a bee line of a bullet just as much as a bullet of a bee line coming for them too.

BIG BELLE: They're dead, you can't tell them anything.

ORPH: Excuse me, I used the present tense which in my experience doesn't preclude them not being deceased.

(That is ignored as much as anyone there can.

HAMMER turns to the other men at the barricade for moral assistance, but McINTOSH is really dozing and HORRIE is now engrossed again in practising late cuts)

HAMMER: (to anyone re DADDY) Mind you, I'm not saying I didn't know this one. A glutton for fish'n'chips with vinegar and a double Coke with two sugars extra, if I remember, but still lived to a ripe old age. Hear tell his missus kept getting in the family way.

DADDY: (corny, piping up) She kept getting' in every bastard's way.

(HORRIE is wickedly signalling to CHINA for a burst of the headlight beam that cruelly settles on DADDY again.

When it does so, DADDY comes to the alert with a strangled cry, gets up to stand shielding his eyes from it. As alarmed as he is, he forces himself to stand before it defiantly.

A sudden P.A. bursts over all:)

37

P.A. OVER: 'On the first count of the murder of the Aboriginal male, Ronald McIntosh, alias Cheeky, how do you find the first defendant? Not guilty as charged?'

McINTOSH: (driven out of sleep) Yeah!

P.A. 'Guilty as not charged?'

McINTOSH: Yeah!

P.A. 'On the first count of the malicious wounding of the Aboriginal girl, Stephanie Duke, how do you find the first defendant? Not guilty as charged? Guilty as not charged?'

McINTOSH: What'd I do?!

HAMMER: (threatening to go up lane) China, you shove that right up your mickey!

DADDY: (couldn't agree more) Cut it out, you mad buggers. Tone it down, turn 'em off.
    (pointing at barricade as though she was there by McINTOSH)
Orphie, you p.o.q. and get on home.

McINTOSH: What've I done now?

    (The headlights go off.

    But they are now having to fend off the bugs that have come with the headlights, scratching themselves)

ORPH: (at HAMMER) What about some insect spray you mean.

HAMMER: No, I didn't.

ORPH: Yes, you did. You said we're meeting out here, but did you bother with the antihistamine? What I've said at work if there was more histamine there wouldn't be the need for so much histamine and less need for cancer cells. But do you care?

HAMMER: No.

ORPH: That's precisely why histamine is losing the battle.

BIG BELLE: ('yeah') I blow up like a balloon, you know.

HORRIE: Anyone notice the difference?

BIG BELLE: I'll really clobber you, sport.

HAMMER: (re DADDY again) Anyway, I'll grant you a certain resemblance, that's all. And who's to say that hasn't come out of a lump of modelling clay?

BIG BELLE: Are you being serious or fucking factitious?

DADDY: (fearful repeat) F'itious!

(In rhythm with his increasing agitation, the 'headlights' now begin dipping on and off to feed his rising fright)

DADDY: Eh watcha! Eh? Go home, Orph! Pissorf, y'dingoes!

(As if in mocking response the PA gives another burst:)

P.A.: 'On the first count of the murder of the Aboriginal male, Ronald McIntosh, alias Cheeky, how do you find the first defendant? Guilty as not charged? Not guilty as charged? On the count of the malicious wounding of the young woman, Stephanie Duke, how do you find the first defendant? Not guilty as charged? Guilty as not charged? On the count of the malicious wounding of the Aboriginal male, Warren Tighe, whom you thought we had forgotten, how do you find the defendant? Guilty as not charged? Not guilty as charged?'

DADDY: (squinting at HAMMER) No more trouble, eh? Call it a day, orright?

(As if in compliance, the headlights go off)

DADDY: Not as quick on my pins as I used to be, eh? Thursdays. Real bugger of a day, pay days. You couldn't see me for dust come pay days. Always trouble, pay days. Queues every rotten where.
  (then, doubling over with pain)
Feel someone's got a good one in... dunno how.

HAMMER: Oh... *please*. Listen, old man, I'm hurting. They're scratching. We're all hurting and scratching. But go on, get it off your concave chest. Say you remember me, so I can deny it to a few around here I could name. You got a problem with pay day? I haven't got a problem with pay day. Anyone got a problem with pay day?

McINTOSH: When's ours?

HAMMER: I've no problem with pay day because I can't remember when the last one was.

DADDY: (trying to be friendly*)* You from the court?
  (chortle)
A bloke had t'take up collecting empties for an excuse to look in on the Imperial this arvo.

HORRIE: It's morning, Pop.

DADDY: ('no') It was this arvo when I peeked into the Imperial. I asked any of us blacklisted? That bastard man Jarvis, he said no. So I asked him straight out: oh yeah, so why's we blacklisted when the barney started? He had nothing to come back at a man with. So there you go, eh?
  (*then*)
I gettin' on your hammer?

40

HAMMER: You're not getting on my hammer. I'm Hammer. I am on my own hammer.

ORPH: You go on before it all becomes too late, Daddy. May I call you Daddy since I've never come at calling my own Daddy, Daddy.

DADDY: A bloke doesn't have to go all shirty just cors a bloke's getting on 'is hammer. Worse thing is I know a bloke'll get on your hammer sooner or later. I dunno. I come into town and, blow me down, next thing I'm gettin' on some b's hammer. Pay days's the worst.
    (then)
Y'know the last white boss fellah I had left me a note? Way back.
    (stops with the sudden thought)
I told you this one?

HAMMER: The note read, 'Daddy, draw your wages. You're giving us all the shits.' He wasn't *the* boss. He was the foreman. You were mending fences. This fence here as a matter of fact. I know all about it, but what I want to know is
    (daggers at the others)
how do you?

DADDY: No, no. Left it on his desk right there under his la-de-dah dictaphone, eh?

HAMMER: *(gives up)* Forget it.

DADDY: Never forget that lah-de-dah dictaphone in them days.
    (suddenly stops and shivers)
Strike it, left my pullie behind. Got the shake of the old bones. Don't worry about it.

HAMMER: We're not.

41

BIG BELLE: Yes, we are. You carry on shivering, Daddy.

DADDY: Thanks. I told my Orphie, I said, that's what pubs're for, keepin' a blue off the streets. If pubs don't keep a knuckle up off the streets, it's a bloody waste of good drinkin' space, eh? Y'don't go…

> *(and suddenly it seems his whole life is centred around having to fight off bull ants. He starts off slowly hitting at them, then increases in intensity until it seems he is heading for a stroke or some such)*

HAMMER: Shissake, don't go having a fit on us.

DADDY: Bloody bullies. You ever collected enough of bullies to have a feast, eh?

HAMMER: Old man, are you making an observation about bull ants?

DADDY: What else wouldja wanna get enough of to eat from?

HAMMER: I wouldn't have a clue.

DADDY: State of today. Y'ain't alone. I tell my lot: whatcha cashing those cheques for down at the store? Good red meat right under yer feet. Eh? I right?

HAMMER: Is that a joke?

DADDY: She listenin', my Orph?

HAMMER: I don't know. Is she?

BIG BELLE: Of course she is, Daddy. Aren't you, Orph?

ORPH: (not buying it) I try not to let anyone see me moving my lips in case it is assumed I am talking to one of them. A lot of make-up artists do, but I never have.

DADDY: I got bitten by a nest of bullies just after I was born. My old Dad was keepin' them cors he like to eat 'em on toast… bit of the old Veggie keeps 'em stuck on top, too right. It was in the back of a buckboard on the way to hospital. Where I was born, I mean. Not the toast, although sometimes you couldn't get him away if there was a bit of quince jam kicking around the place. Bullies and quince jam, it didn't matter who was being born. He liked a bit of cheese on top too.

> *(stops, ponders a feeling of sadness, but cannot put his finger on the cause of it; then:)*

Moree. Lived here all my life and never seen so much trouble, except that time those young noongs come here on that Freedom Ride thingo. Good day, that. Gave the local white fellahs buggery. Who was that, eh?

HAMMER: Charlie Perkins.

DADDY: No, just cherry pickin', thanks. Anyways, back at the Home, I told m'mate Belle. I said I'd be raising my hand in that court, too right. I'll tell that judge in no uncertain terms. Our boys was just having a bit of fun, finishing off the few brown ones, that's all. Anything up with that? What's uppin' an' aimin' an' pullin' a trigger got to do with that?

HAMMER: Do you want the historical answer?

DADDY: I'll tell that bugger of a judge I tried me best to get the White lairs to pull their heads in. Our young'uns too. What more can a man do?

HAMMER: Do you want the *hysterical* answer?

> *(But DADDY has turned off. HAMMER finds himself without moral support from any of the others. He sits on his haunches as near as he dares get to DADDY and is utterly discouraged.*

43

There is a surly silence all round.

Finally, HORRIE faces up again. McINTOSH jumps down from barricade to act as wicket keeper. HORRIE gestures up lane to CHINA to let another ball fly. It comes by sound effect, obviously rips through HORRIE's forward defense and knocks McINTOSH backwards)

HORRIE: (down at him) Moree's answer to Don Bradman.

McINTOSH: I slipped.

HORRIE: Sure.

McINTOSH: They always aim for making the old eyes water.

(but HORRIE has engendered an energy suddenly in the atmosphere)

HORRIE: There's this other one I heard outside of bits of paper. Once upon a time in a far-off Aboriginal land an elder probably called Daddy was still the best hunter because he had to best hunting dog. One day he was out after a big roo and the dog took off after it. He waited and waited, but the dog never came back. Old Daddy soon slid down the hunting order of merit. After seven years, he was out as usual relegated to digging up yams with the women when a tiny puppy ran out of the bush. Old Daddy grabbed it, and started shouting, 'Chasing that roo for seven years's made me dog as skinny as a rake.' So he took the pup back to camp and laid him up. They all laughed at him too, but he soon became the hot shot hunter again because the dog with a bit of tucker under its belt was soon as good as it ever was.

BIG BELLE: (still 'at' HAMMER) Yeah, moral to that. Feed us morning coffee, and we'll stop barking.

DADDY: They used to have a bus what ended down this lane here. Nobody got on it and nobody got off, so they ended it.

44

Things were a bit more democratic when that bus came all the way down here. Y'wanna know something else?

(Another long pause. It allows HAMMER to get up the desire to carry on)

HAMMER: All right, count me in.

DADDY: The place you wanted to go never seemed where it was goin', eh? Don't get me wrong. It was always goin' buzzin' around all over the place, that bus, but, see, its bugger of a sign board never changed. D'you know what that bugger of a sign board said?

BIG BELLE: (to be polite) What did it say, Daddy?

DADDY: That's what I was askin'.

(She gives up)

DADDY: They reckoned it always said Here. Comin' or goin', they said it always said Here. I never looked. I never cared where I was goin' in those days. I never cared if I was going Here or coming back from Here, those days. Comin' or goin', no sweat. Like now, you take me, eh?

HAMMER: (suddenly interested) What about you?

DADDY: I'm waiting here because that bus's still the fastest way to get to Endeavour Lane even if you don't know if it's gonna turn up an' you don't know where it's goin'.

HAMMER: Or if Endeavour Lane's Here.

DADDY: Or if Endeavour Lane's Here. That's spot on, that is. Moree, they say it says now. That's okay by me. It's what I call progress.

ORPH: We are in Moree, Daddy. I've always said if you're ever in doubt you don't have to take the word of whoever sells all the wreathes.

(HAMMER looks at DADDY closely, gets a revelation and finally become fully excited again:)

HAMMER: He really doesn't know where he is! I told you!

BIG BELLE: We could have told you that hours ago.

HAMMER: Nobody do anything!

BIG BELLE: Who'd find something to do?

(HAMMER is thinking, waves for silence, until:)

HAMMER: As I see it, there are three alternatives. All of which aren't worth a pig's bum, I admit. One: he will show his hand by fidgeting rather than really shake by the possible onset of Parkinson's, in which case we will do nothing. Two, he will show a steady hand by putting it out and demanding to see how we intend to depict him. We will do nothing. Three, he will show his hand with an accusing finger by demanding a handout for depicting him or he's not moving except for the Parkinsons. I prefer the last possibility as I'm sure one of you will cover me being a bit short this morning.

BIG BELLE: Yeah, you can open your mouth, but not your hip pocket.

HAMMER: Ignoring that, it boils down to which one of you has the social conscience to do the needful...

(He waits for a reply, any reply. But he cannot prevent DADDY from getting upset again)

DADDY: Someone say Orphie?

46

HAMMER: Sorry, old guy, there's no Orphie around here. Not that type of Orphie anyway.

DADDY: (calling) ORPHIE?

HAMMER: Hey!

DADDY: You say something about my Orphie?

HAMMER: (going along with it) Oh, her.

DADDY: I told her straight. Orphie, y'oughta keep out of them utes. Keep right out of them bars. How many time do I have to bash her ear? What's she doin' in the pub anyway?
  (*again*)
ORPHIE?
  (*appealing to the women*)
She changed out of that singlet job, tits hanging all over the place, eh? I told her straight, you wanta keep away from the police, you go n' change. Magistrate'll get his eye poked out if you lean over his bench, ha ha. She'd a good kid, but. She's all I got left.

BIG BELLE: She'll be along.

DADDY: What'd she want to go into the pub with them for, anyway, banned? I'm banned. I'm always banned, but y'don't see me going in there. What's wrong with havin' a few sips outside round the back. That pisses you off well have a piss up against the pub wall, what I say. Show 'em who's really boss deep down.

  (*He stops and there is a strange hiatus*)

HAMMER: Anyone like to help, please feel free to.

DADDY: (indicating HORRIE) I know what he is.
  (*holds out hand for palm reading*)
How much for the full go?

47

(HORRIE rises to the challenge of being mistaken for a fortune teller. He grabs DADDY's hand roughly, looks and pretends)

HORRIE: You ever been to Mars?

DADDY: Which side of the Murray's that on?

HORRIE: I see the gullies and run-offs of Mars.

DADDY: Oh, Mars.

HORRIE: I see a day in court.

(Seeing the possibilities in this, HAMMER shoves HORRIE aside, takes over DADDY's palm:)

HAMMER: And I see the tracks of the great serpent and, boy, has He had to hop over the breaks in this life line. Now, here, that's not a slip. That's a watering hole.

DADDY: (chuckle) Had a quick sip before I come here. How did you see that there?

HORRIE: I see your young'uns going hammer and tongs at it in the pub…

DADDY: Which pub's that?

HORRIE: The Imperial.

DADDY: It was the Imperial!

HORRIE: Moree.

DADDY: It was Moree! Jeez, you're good!

HORRIE: You are kissing the publican's ring and trying to bugger the publican's alsatian.

DADDY: Eh?

HAMMER: If that 'eh?' means 'go on', I do go on following these furrows...
(he whips out another piece of paper to read from)
I see you swinging by your neck in your cell. You look quite gay really for what is referred to as an Aboriginal in custody. They're saying oh crap and we only scrubbed the concrete floor six months ago. I see... here and here... how you're off to another court, another inquiry. But the snag is, Daddy, no court room's big enough for you, sorry. You have to be mucking around here, when you should be getting justice there.

DADDY: They can all piss off!

(He tries to withdraw his palm but HAMMER keeps hold of it)

HAMMER: Looking ahead, I can arrange for one of us to visit you in prison and cut you down.
(quoting some unknown old joke)
"Evil effects from tomorrow".

(and drops the old man's hand, turns away)

DADDY: (to his back) Nice to have someone to wait with. Who're you here for?

HAMMER: (daggers at others) It might be that we don't have a clue.

DADDY: ('but') I heard shots. Looked out of m'window and there's smoke rising. Shots and smoke and pay day. Bugger of a combination, that. Now where'd that palm-readin' gypsy fellah go? Didn't pay.

49

(Seizing opportunity, HAMMER furtively puts out his hand to get paid for the palm reading. DADDY struggles to find something to pay him with and finally holds out a coin. On HAMMER mitting it, the women are outraged)

BIG BELLE: Hey!

HAMMER: *(innocently)* What?

BIG BELLE: What a greedy pig!

HAMMER: *(re-taking DADDY's hand as cover-up)* The mount on Queen Moon. The small lines leading to here, here and here, like some old bus signboard says. Vast journeys of the mind. Let's call it a natural diet not malnutrition. Nothing beats a staple diet of sour sobs.

BIG BELLE: The greedy pig bit me for ten only this morning.

ORPH: Me yesterday too and he hadn't cleaned out all those cows internals from under his fingernails neither.

HAMMER: (scandalised) That was plain ordinary dirt!
  (back to DADDY's palm)
This pronounced bump indicates great economic development coming your way as long as you agree to be moved to another cell location.

DADDY: (looking) Think that's my old boil.

BIG BELLE: Greedy pig! Not even four of a kind would make me want to stay and watch this.

(She huffs off yet again)

ORPH: And I just want to say that any reading of any palm is the same dead or alive.

HORRIE: (stopping out of interest) So what?

ORPH: It shows you how useless it is, so there.

(She huffs off following BIG BELLE.

As a matter of pride, HAMMER perseveres with DADDY's palm regardless:)

HAMMER: I see a beginning in that back of the old buckboard.

DADDY: What buckboard's that?

HAMMER: The one you talked about.

DADDY: Did I blab about that, eh?
    (*chortles*)
Still got the splinters in m'bum.

HAMMER: Your Daddy-before-you is smacking your little bot as hard as he dares, but there you are, going blue as the blowies. You start bawling out to your parents I've come to make us Kamilroi mob warlike and warrior again, taking its orders of ham sandwiches left, right and centre out of the Ned Kelly bar and into the streets.

DADDY: I met you before?

HAMMER: (re the money) So I'm in my rights to take this?

DADDY: Reckon.

HAMMER: Out of interest, who tattooed this X-marks-the-spot on the palm of your other hand?

DADDY: I don't see any X-marks-the-watcha.

51

HAMMER: Never mind. Our main concern now is being here in Endeavour Lane and either waiting for, or too late to do anything about, the spilling out of the dust-up from the Ned Kelly's bar to here to set up a barricade much like a barricade you might see somewhere close by if you happened to look around.

DADDY: Blood oath!

HAMMER: Snag is, which?, are you coming to the rescue or gone to the dogs?
  (*looking around*)
Anyone tell from the empties? Horrie?

McINTOSH: I'm good at empties. What'm I looking for?

HAMMER: Check it out.

> (*McINTOSH looks around the nearby lanes, nudges a few empties with his foot, returns to barricade*)

McINTOSH: I dunno.

HAMMER: Dads?

DADDY: Buggered if I know what you're on about. I'm just here tryin' to mind me own business.

> (*He gets up slowly, drags his overnight back off towards up the lane. He is obviously about to leave but stops to express thought of:*)

DADDY: My old Dad reckoned it was the fault of that Hayley's Comet, bludger of a thing.

> (*Pause, while HAMMER looks at HORRIE, who refuses to have anything to do with rising to this.*)

HAMMER: (leadenly) Halley's Comet.

DADDY: Halley's bloody Comet. Real bugger of a thing. Time before that, it brought the whitefellah what named Botany Bay when we didn't know any Botany Bay, like. Same with Moree. If it wasn't for Halley's Comet where would Botany Bay be? Or Moree? Instead we end up with that real mongrel of a publican up at the Imperial. That Halley's never did us Kamilrois any good.

(He obviously sees BIG BELLE and ORPH up the lane ahead of him)

DADDY: Not bad sorts, them. They plainclothes coppers?

HAMMER: There's no coppers.

DADDY: (explanation) See that's what I'm saying. You see sheilas around here, follow them. They know a thing or two about buses. (*then*)
Hey, jeez, haven't lost m'ticket, have I?
 (*scrambles back to look among the debris*)
You seen a ticket?

HAMMER: (wearil*y)* No ticket.

DADDY: You think m'Orphie's got it?

HAMMER: I would not know her.

DADDY: She ought to be thundering back soon. When she's got her back up, those white larries better not start monkeyin' around.
 (getting worked up again)
A man can't get to court without 's ticket!

HORRIE: *There is no fucking ticket!*

DADDY: (searching wallet again) Had the bludger in here...

HAMMER: Look, look…!

*(He grabs the wallet and the ticket flutters to the ground.
DADDY swoops on it with huge relief.)*

DADDY: Man's getting a real dill, ain't I?

HAMMER: Look at the date, shit it!

*(HAMMER grabs it off him, looks at it, throws it back in
disgust)*

HAMMER: Cheap printing trick.

(It settles down to another long silence.

*HORRIE shrugs, goes back to taking cricket guard.
Motions down lane for CHINA to send another
imaginary ball down. It comes by with its sound effect.
Obviously a bouncer. HORRIE ducks. McINTOSH is
knocked off the barricade.*

*By now, BIG BELLE and ORPHIE have returned so far
but not all the way)*

HAMMER: Why, ladies, couldn't get past China?

*(Surlily they refuse to answer, until ORPH turns her
anger onto HAMMER:)*

ORPH: How would you know? Have you even ever inspected
a coffin?

HAMMER: Good point, whatever it is.
  (swings back to DADDY)
Forgery or not, you see, Daddy… nevertheless all of us here
have known the quiet madness and badness and their
unsadness.

BIG BELLE: Leave him alone, can't you?

HAMMER: But, Dads mate, as a group you can see how we are collectively urging you to return to the old people's home they have had your name down for ever since you were born. Be satisfied with that, why not?

BIG BELLE: (trying to be kind) See, Daddy, we've got our own Daddy or supposed to have. He's not due until…

   (She looks around for help)

HAMMER: Somewhere early in the second act, if the script development goes according to plan.

BIG BELLE: (at HAMMER) Not ever if we have to wait on you.

HAMMER: That's so mean. Yet do I pull rank? I do not.
   (*and*)
So you're a bit late, Pops. Or a bit early. Whatever, I tell you what… you pop back next year and we might have something for you. Can't be fairer than that.

   (He leans back against the barricade as though having delivered the coup de grace, and ssh's any movement as he waits for DADDY's reply.

   There is a long fidgeting pause, during which DADDY only sinks nearer to falling into a doze again. Finally, BIG BELLE points out the old man's tiredness:)

BIG BELLE: Look at him!

HAMMER: What?

BIG BELLE: You just recognise what we think of you.

HAMMER: I pong. I stink. I am the sneaky wombat peeing on any plate of food you care to name. Satisfied?

(The women wait, dissatisfied)

HAMMER: All right, I tell you what. If he's got one objection… just one… we'll call the whole thing off. Not only that, we'll certainly think about calling the whole thing off.

(Finally he gets grudging acceptance.

DADDY, in the meantime, has gone back to dozing off, and HAMMER has to unceremoniously capture his attention by lifting his head from the overnight bag)

HAMMER: It's like this, Dads. One day your hair is growing grey, and your people are thinning out. You're suddenly gone past fifty. The white boss cockeys are calling it 1838.

(HORRIE eagerly takes yet another piece of paper HAMMER has taken from a pocket and reads from it:)

HORRIE: And one of these fine days in a far-off Aboriginal land you find yourself with some half a hundred of your people on a ridge above Myall Creek not too far from Moree, certainly within the same coast-to-coast, and you're all hot and dusty and looking down on Dangar's Station with its model cookhouse and bunkhouses out back and you think, why not trade a few of your girlies for a few favours in rum-bottle shape and a bit of that shade and a bit of that flesh on the bone them dogs down there are gutsing themselves? Where's the worry?

HAMMER: And that's how it all got started, see, Daddy. So it's no good waiting here and now.
    (hams a Moses-type figure)
Daddy of the Kamilroi Moree mob, do not go down to Dangar Station today! Do not go into Moree! Do not near the Imperial Hotel! Nix on the Sydney bus!
    (stops himself with amazement)

Why'd I say 'Sydney'?

BIG BELLE: Who's listening?

HAMMER: Old man, now would be a good time to just up and boodle off to immortality.

ORPH: You see, Daddy, you mightn't be able to feel immortality but it'll feel you. Some might sneer and call it a slab, but someone has to clean you up.

> *(Even she stops when DADDY holds up his hand for silence)*

DADDY: Gonna put m'head down for a bit... Keep an eye out, eh?

HAMMER: *(gives up, dusts hands)* Hopeless. He's all yours. I wash my hands of him.

BIG BELLE: You've already wiped your hands *on* him, mongrel you.

ORPH: What gets my goat is we're all being rotten to the elderly!

HORRIE: You're being rotten to the elderly every time you doll them up for the funeral.

HAMMER: (trying to pacify) People, let's think of our commitment to the ghosts of our acting careers.

HORRIE: (lewd) Ghosts have no fannies, therefore no commitment.

> *(DADDY opens his eyes, wide awake, before the women can take issue with this, and:)*

DADDY: No good.

(They stop to listen but get no more out of him)

HAMMER: Is he objecting already?

DADDY: (slapping at bites) Bloody bullies, you can't beat them down this lane.

HAMMER: No pertinent objection registered.
 (snaps fingers)
Pillow. Blanket!

> *(ORPH, having volunteered, now has to cast around for something to act as a blanket. She decides on the 'wicket' piece of cardboard, puts it over the old man)*

HAMMER: Any objections?

DADDY: No way, eh.

HAMMER: Registered.

ORPH: Comfy now?

DADDY: They call a man Daddy. Dunno why.

ORPH: I'm Orph. You can call me Orph.

DADDY: M'daughter's called Orph. I call her Orphie or Orph, too. Bugger orph, ha ha.

> *(but is cut off when the headlights high beam flashes back on to shine in his eyes again from off. He is blinded, thrashes about. They shut off just as suddenly as they assaulted him)*

DADDY: Hey, that wasn't the bus, was it?

HAMMER: Hey, don't start that again!

DADDY: No, fair kick up the quoit, was that the bus?
Anyone see m'little Orph get off? Red hair?
  (*no one is going to bite*)
Don't ask me where she got the red hair from. I must've eaten
beetroot th'night before, eh, ha ha?

HAMMER: (now aggressive) Are you *griping* now?

DADDY: Me, gripin'?

HAMMER: Are you objecting to red hair now?
  (*indicating ORPH*)
You complaining about her red hair?

DADDY: Eh?

HAMMER: No 'eh'. Are you objecting to the way we set up
the barricade or what the hell China's doing up there... well,
you're allowed to object to those... but are you otherwise
objecting?

DADDY: Eh?

HAMMER: Is he objecting?

BIG BELLE: Keep *your* objectionable shirt on.

HAMMER: Okay, we'll say no objection. Also, griping is not
necessarily objecting.

DADDY: (butting in) Had t'ask the doc's advice before he'd let
me beetle off to Sydney as a witness. I says to him, they say a
bloke might be dangerously ill, and he says, naw, Daddy,
you're just dangerously old. Hadta chortle.

> (*DADDY laughs at his own joke, as do the women, but
> comes down with the beginning of a coughing fit and has
> to stop. While he wins to control it -- but only just -- he*

59

starts beckoning to McINTOSH who reluctantly gets down from barricade to go near him)

DADDY: Be a mate an' go down the lane a bit n' see if you can see my daughter Orph coming, eh? Your legs're younger than mine.

McINTOSH: Sorry, dude, really busy.

HAMMER: (urging him) Keep him sweet.

McINTOSH: No laying into me fee?

HAMMER: No laying into your fee.

McINTOSH: Here I go then.

> *(He does a lightning tap dance. Stops as though mission accomplished.)*

McINTOSH: He feel sweeter now?

BIG BELLE: Look, go and have a proper look.

McINTOSH: (spooked) I'd rather you laid into me fee.

HAMMER: We will if you don't go.

> *(McINTOSH reluctantly moves off down the lane)*

ORPH: (after him) Beware of the speeding bullet around about the 56.75 metre mark if the slide rule in my head has anything to do with it. Keep the knees bent.
   (*and to BIG BELLE*)
I have that slide rule in my will, you know.

BIG BELLE: Come again?

ORPH: ('simple') To remember to take it out.

60

DADDY: (after McINTOSH) Good young fellah, that. All m'boys are.

(There is a silence while they wait. They don't have to do so for long... McINTOSH returns. He could not have gone more than a few metres, walks past them all and mans the barricade again)

McINTOSH: *(surlily)* Looked everywhere.

(Accusing silence. Before someone can gather the energy to tackle him, they are again abused by a P.A. burst:)

P.A.: 'On the first count of the murder of the Aboriginal male, Ronald Cheeky McIntosh, how do you find the first defendant? Not guilty as charged; otherwise guilty as not charged? Can we hurry this along, please? On the first count of the toss-up between grievous malicious wounding and the piss-weak ordinary malicious wounding of the Aboriginal woman, Stephanie Duke, how do you find the three defendants? Not guilty as charged; otherwise guilty as not charged?'

(It is depressing all round; HAMMER tries a rally of spirits:)

HAMMER: Since one of you is going to have to pay the Council for this look-see, me being temporarily a bit short...

(gets drowned out again by another P.A. burst)

P.A.: 'On the first count of the toss-up between murder and malicious wounding of the Aboriginal male, Warren Rocky Tighe how do you find the first defendant? Did he drop first or don't we send him in at first drop?...'

(HAMMER gives up again. He readily complies with HORRIE making gestures for another piece of paper)

61

HORRIE: (reading) …There was this once in a far-off Aboriginal land when this old boy comes across a young lubra in the scrub. He tells her how lucky she is; only rarely did the kindly spirit of maiden-heads like him show himself to passing maidens. Golly gosh, what should I do, she asked. Well, if she allowed him to have his way with her, she could have anything she wanted. Oh, yes, please, she said. When he was finished he walked away. Excuse me, Mr Kindly Spirit, what about that everything I could wish for?, she called. He turned and asked her how old she was. Seventeen she told him. "Ain't that a bit old to be going around believing in kindly spirits?', he said.

DADDY: (*piping up*) That reminds me of m'boy. Poor little bugger, real crook all his life. He just kept bleedin' like a stuck pig. His chest or arms or legs, see, they'd open up and away he goes, bleeding like that stuck pig. Think we could stop it, even with our own bush medicine? Be buggered. One day he was orright… the next he was gone. I said to young Cheeky McIntosh and his crew, I said, now you're all my boys. Just keep your meat pickers off m'little Orphie. Orphie's all I got left.

(At this, there is a pause of not knowing how to react)

HAMMER: He is emoting, not objecting.

HORRIE: From what I can see, seems to me he's got no balls.

BIG BELLE: That's a really shitty thing to say.

HORRIE: Well, you've got to have no equipment when you lose your mother giving birth to you in the back of a buckboard, and then lose your only son with what's got to be leukemia... and all you end up saying to the world is 'Orphie's all I got left'.

BIG BELLE: The important thing, Daddy, is to remember you're important to someone.

DADDY: *(up at BIG BELLE)* Aw, you remind me of a piece I know.

BIG BELLE: Call me Belle, Daddy.

DADDY: I know a Belle. Matron back at the Home. Legs like piano legs, too. Same size bra as you, too, I reckon. Same parachute, ha ha.

BIG BELLE: (but pleased) Really?

DADDY: Real pain in the backside, she is.

BIG BELLE: *(still pleased)* Really?

DADDY: Kind, eh? She gave me this overnight bag to take to Sydney.

BIG BELLE: How nice.

DADDY: Pongs a bit, but; the bluebottles always trying to blow her, dunno why. She told a man how to make a stink bomb in case something happens in court. She wiped her armpit and said 'Use this in an emergency'. I reckon she's a bit sweet on a bloke.

(He starts coughing alarmingly.)

ORPH: (outcry) He isn't well!

BIG BELLE: Orph, if he's got this far with this lot, he'll survive to be Australia's first man on Mars.

DADDY: Orphie?

(Instantly, there is another headlight assault on him. DADDY struggles to fight against it and the mounting fit of coughing. He strains to see HORRIE as the

Imperial's publican:)

DADDY: This is a public bar, bloody Jarvis! We're got a right...!

(There is a burst of an all-in pub fight breaking out. He shouts, struggles against it:)

DADDY: You get on home, Orphie!

(ORPH goes to hurry over to him but is blinded herself of course. She trips fully over him and lies prone. HORRIE quickly motion for the headlight beam to be switched off.

DADDY is dazed for a moment before noticing ORPH swooned there)

DADDY: ORPHIE...!

(He scrambles towards her, collapses over her.

She panics, struggling to get out from under him, manages to stand. But DADDY just lies there. She is helpless to know what to do with him.

The others gather around her, looking down at DADDY motionless there. They are all appalled, but equally not knowing what to do with him)

BIG BELLE: (at ORPH) What'd you do that for?

ORPH: (outcry) Don't ask me! I'm used to being on top of bodies!

(General lighting fades, while P.A. rises)

P.A. 'On the day of the slaughter, the blacks were crying and moaning the same as a lot of children would cry; there were

64

many who could not walk; the whole party then went away taking the blacks with them. the station foreman Kilmeister rode in front and took the rope to which the blacks were tied and the rest of his men followed after and on each side of the natives. Kilmeister and his men took them away. The rope was a long tether rope. There was one old man called Daddy amongst the blacks; he was the eldest of the lot. Nobody knew where he had come from or why he was there.'

(end Act 1)

Act 2

(The barricade setting is as before, except now they have dusted down a battered old couch for DADDY.

BIG BELLE is dabbing his forehead with a damp cloth. The others are sitting around watching remorsefully. By DADDY is a bottle of beer.

The long silence is punctuated only by BIG BELLE's cooing at him, who is getting a bit confused with her midwife's life by telling him to 'Push' when she means breathe-out.

Finally, HAMMER comes over, lifts his hand and is about to stick a pin in it)

HAMMER: If he complains about this, it's a pain not an objection.

(He sticks the pin in. DADDY doesn't move. HAMMER tries again. Still nothing. He takes a tissue from his pocket and sticks it into DADDY's nostrils.

No reaction.

HAMMER next goes to his feet, takes off one of his shoes. He reels back. BIG BELLE gasps with what she sees. The others crowd around to see what the trouble is)

HORRIE: My God, if that's not the Syph, I'm still in the market.

McINTOSH: Somebody must have laid right into him.

HAMMER: Must have been a stray. Point of entry, see.

BIG BELLE: A stray what?

HAMMER: If I knew, it'd only give him an unfair advantage.

BIG BELLE: (accusatory) Something else stinks around here.

ORPH: Oh, I don't know. My boss finds onsetting gangrene quite toothsome. Question of your personal taste in air sprays, really.

BIG BELLE: (waving that off) I asked what stray.

HAMMER: How do I know? A bee called a wasp in a heavy metal jacket, say, buzzing. Take your pick. Up on a ridge over Myall Creek, they lined them all up. Or down here, a young hoon gets the old Winchester 30/30 out from under the front seat of his Dad's ute and lets a few fly. A stray? There's a lot of them going around parts of Australia.

> *(He finally overcomes his repulsion to tickle DADDY's sole. BIG BELLE giggles. He stops. She stops. He does so again; she giggles again, then stops when he stops.)*

HAMMER: If he put his hand in the fire they built at the barricade, would you?

> *(and walks away and sits idly. The others follow. The exception is HORRIE who edges over to take the bottle of beer.*
>
> *Before he can lift it, DADDY's hand flops over to fall proprietorially onto the bottle. HORRIE has a tug of war with the old man, but gives up. He looks at DADDY closely, waves his hand in front of the old man's eyes, but gets no reaction)*

HORRIE: That's one who might actually take it with him.

> *(and returns to practising his pull shots. Long pause)*

67

BIG BELLE: He scared seven bells of hell out of me, keeling over like that.

ORPH: What are we going to *do*? I know we have some spare stretchers at work but they're all taken up or Sundays are their days off.

HAMMER: Did anyone loosen his belt? The manual says, if anyone keels over on you or... *(weak laugh)* ...gets keeled, they say step one is you leap in and go the belt.

McINTOSH: That's on the notice boards of all the detention centres you come across.

ORPH: There's not much you can do until they're well and truly gone. A bit of blush, maybe, but, honestly, I don't know where they get 'well' in 'well and truly' from, and never have. But if I did it's only based on scientific evidence.

HAMMER: 'Scientific evidence', what?

ORPH: What's what?

HAMMER: That.

ORPH: That what?

HAMMER: What has that got to do with this foot here?

ORPH: That's not my foot. It would be well and truly in the disinfecting box by now.

> *(HAMMER has to give up again. He goes back to goes back to DADDY, takes his pulse)*

HAMMER: Heart? Like a baby's on the breast. Anything else comes with the genes, right?, and not my fault.

ORPH: Now that we're talking scientific facts. I read somewhere that as far back as 1788 they've been trying to induce their strands of DNA into us. I too doubted that at first but, 1788 being from the word go, it's safer to believe that than go back and check. I think there you have enough said right there.

(She clams up. There is a long quizzical pause)

BIG BELLE: (at the foot) I still want to know what's caused that.

HAMMER: Who can tell? Scar tissue, old broken bones? Old kneeling-before injury?
  (at ORPH)
You've done CPR.

ORPH: I'm not lipping my orals near a near dead man I don't know. Mind you, speaking of facts, if you can get them before too much damage, there's supposed to be a window of opportunity when they go sterile two to ten minutes after cadaverous rigor mortis. Then you might conceivably lip your orals on CPR on the road to being too late anyway. Always thought that interesting.

BIG BELLE: Look, all you have to do is blow instead of suck.

ORPH: You do it. I wouldn't want to give him my cold.

BIG BELLE: Do I have to do everything around here?

(But she does not move. Long pause.

HAMMER selects another piece of paper from his pocket, gives it to HORRIE, who accepts it quite readily, knowing his job is to get things moving again.

He reads:)

HORRIE: Once upon a time in a far-off Aboriginal land, there were these four brothers. The eldest was the tribe's best at carving; the second at bark painting; the third at magic; and the youngest, a hopeless wanker. One night, the eldest bloke couldn't sleep so he carved a beautiful lubra out of a piece of wood, then fell asleep. Then the second brother woke up, decided to fiddle around and body painted a beautiful lubra fit for a queen, before falling back to sleep. The third woke up and conjured up a beautiful lubra in the dust at his feet and, while he was at it, thought he might as well diddle her before going back to sleep like his other brothers. What he didn't know was that diddling brought her to life. Now that she was alive the beautiful lubra went all female about everybody zizzing away when there she was all naked and alive and painted up, so she kicked the youngest brother awake and gave him a mouth full. Now that he was awake he gave her one across the moosh for waking him up.

BIG BELLE: Hey! Enough of that!

HORRIE: Lady, listen and learn something.
    (*carries on reading*)
So next morning the three elder brothers saw how she had turned out and started a barney about who owned her. Finally, they brought in the wise man called Daddy. The old man listened to their claims, then gave his verdict: 'She belongs to the youngest one. You three treated her like a real lady, but at least he treated her properly and gave her one for trying to flash her fruit when a man's trying to get a little shut-eye'.

   *(BIG BELLE is ready to take on either HAMMER or
   HORRIE or both)*

BIG BELLE: I've told you before, you keep coming out with rubbish like that and you'll get a real lady's knuckle sandwich.

HAMMER: Look, mes enfants, I know what going on. He could have keeled over anywhere in Moree. In Moree, there're doing it all the time. You go up to the end of this lane, it's like watching dead leaves in a gale.

BIG BELLE: He's a just an ordinary old bloke, and you're picking on him.

McINTOSH: (butting in) You ask me, if they peg, they peg. It's like getting laid into. The one minute you're going okay, the next it hurts like buggery.

BIG BELLE: Okay, okay. Lay off it.

HAMMER: You think he's got problems? I'm fifty next week.

BIG BELLE: Boo hoo. You should have thought of that before you done Daddy down.

HAMMER: Done Daddy down. Rather like that. Borrowable? Anyway, I did not done Daddy down. When I get down to the penning of Moree and 1982, it will fall to my lot to administer certain circumstances. You say walk to an old man and he steps out in front of a car. Who do you apologise to? Alternatively, to whom do you apologise? You don't know. All you know is there's damage to the front fender. All you can prove is perhaps I didn't finish fifth grade.

BIG BELLE: Yeah, and all I want to know is after...
    (*indicates presence of DADDY*)
... are you going to stick to this getting-the-feel-of-the-place crud?

HAMMER: *(shocked)* What's wrong with it?

BIG BELLE: It's about as real as your mother's womb.

HAMMER: That's terribly cheap and nasty.

BIG BELLE: Yeah, and so's your play.

71

HAMMER: Excuse me, do I diminish your work as a midwife just because you refuse to allow more than two contractions?

BIG BELLE Two contractions from your cows and you'd go cross-eyed. It's not even the 25th anniversary of the riot like you claimed.

HAMMER: So we're out by a mere ten years or so. That's what they expect of us. Us getting it wrong just means it's authentic.

BIG BELLE: And it was shotgun pellets not a bullet. I looked it up.

(HAMMER stops on something new)

HAMMER: No, I refuse to entertain this again.

BIG BELLE: Pellets. Pop, pop, not bang-bang. Right?

HAMMER: No, no. Bullets. Pellets don't pack the same theatrical punch as a bullet, so how could it have been pellets? Think about it.

BIG BELLE: Eat this.

ORPH: (suddenly) Do I smell of ether?
   (*this rates as another stopper*)
I had two late bookings last night. I hate to think I bring ether to the party.

HAMMER: (regardless and re DADDY) If he was going to front up, you'd think he'd be able to last the distance at least.

> *(McINTOSH has some sort of headache attack, simply collapses over one of the few bits of the barricade left. He does so not very alarmingly… almost balletically and with a sigh. Accordingly, with the others, it is just another natural thing that has happened)*

BIG BELLE: Stuffit, now what?

HAMMER: Seems like they don't give them concussion tests before they leave police stations anymore.

HORRIE: He'll be jake.

BIG BELLE: Yeah, well, big shot, which one do we help?

> *(She means McINTOSH or DADDY. HAMMER chooses DADDY, points to him)*

HAMMER: Try the fireman's lift.

BIG BELLE: You try it. It takes so kind of crumby four-flusher.

HAMMER: Excuse me, he shuffled in on here. I walked in properly. Now, I don't know why he did, but he did. He' probably been wandering around looking for some place to fall off the perch from the moment he tried to keep playing pool in the middle of the biggest blue this town had seen in years.

BIG BELLE: Who asked for a speech?

HAMMER: (demurely) Can I help that what happens down this country's lanes is at the black heart of it all?

BIG BELLE: Yeah, and what does *that* mean?

HAMMER: I keep telling you: how do I know? I'm just here for a little reconnoitre like you.

BIG BELLE: You wouldn't know what a reconnoitre was if it reconnoitred you. Let's go, Orph.

> *(But ORPH is a bit reluctant to leave the old man in this state)*

ORPH: You know, a trick they should teach in schools is someone putting a mirror up to his nose…?

HAMMER: A mirror is not the point! The point is, this Daddy or that Daddy or any other Daddy has been strapped down over the bulls-eye all his live-long.

(He motions HORRIE to give DADDY another good shake, but still no reaction)

HAMMER: Look, point is, he'll survive. He'll be back there boring the corn flakes out of his young Moree blacks before they turn up at Ned Kelly's bar to drown out the corn flakes.

(He motions them to combine to move DADDY, but they are swamped by a renewed burst from the P.A.)

P.A.: 'Announcement. We regret to announce the delay of the express to Sydney, connecting somehow with the Sydney Harbour Bridge. We apologise for any inconvenience, but the engine driver appears to be drunk and the guard's rung in to say he's got pregnant which seems odd.'

DADDY: *(sitting bolt upright)* Bugger!

(The women screech with pleasure, fling themselves onto him, rough his hair etc.)

DADDY: *(chuckling up at HAMMER)* Hey, mate, knock, knock.

HAMMER: *(great relief)* Who's there?

DADDY: Moree.

HAMMER: Moree who?

DADDY: Call me Daddy. Maurie's me brother.

74

(He laughs at his own joke, and is tickled by the women.
McINTOSH comes awake, leaps down from barricade to
join in the fun:)

McINTOSH: Hey, you remind me of a Kamilroi warrior

DADDY: *(knows it's a joke)* Yeah, and what Kamilroi
warrior?

McINTOSH: A Kamilroi warrior with power.

DADDY: What power?

McINTOSH: The power of a Zulu.

DADDY: Who do?

McINTOSH: You do.

DADDY: What?

McINTOSH: Remind me of a Kamilroi warrior.

DADDY: What Kamilroi ...?

(Etc. BIG BELLE, catching on and happy they're making
progress with him, digs DADDY playfully in the ribs.
The old man sucks air with pain, falls back limp again)

BIG BELLE: What'd I do?

HORRIE: *(*the opportunist*)* Once in this far-off Aboriginal
land, an old man wasn't getting any luck fishing. so he cried out
to the great ancestor Baiame to give him a fish and\ he'd give
half to someone needy. Suddenly a real beautie jumped out of
the water and landed at his feet. It was so big the old man
thought, 'I could live for a week on this bugger. Think I'll wait
until I catch something smaller, then I'll give half of that to

someone needy'. With that, the fish leapt back into the billabong.

(long uncomprehending pause, until DADDY suddenly starts up again)

DADDY: I said to m'daughter Orphie I said, come home and we're go bush and I'll teach you to feel the spirit of your little brother. She said I'm wearing his pyjama top; I'm feeling enough of him already. I said come home and we're go out into the old country and I'll teach you what my Daddy taught my about the Law and she said I've seen enough of the Law down at the dirty rotten station. I said I'll show you and your young mates how to tell a cave painting when you see one. She said we all had to traipse all around the National Art Gallery in Canberra and that was boring enough. I can show you how to reconnect with the bush, I said. She said oh yeah only wearing her little brother's pyjama top? How they go today, eh?

P.A.: 'Announcement. We can announce the capture of the engine driver who ain't half as pissed as his license said he would be, and the guard has proved he's to be made an honest woman of, so we can also announced the transport union's okay with that. Would passengers hoping to catch the bus to the law courts in Sydney stand by in Endeavour Lane so they can be seen as you'd-be-lucky inspirations to us all...'

DADDY: *(revitalised)* Thank buggery.

HAMMER: Panic's over, kiddies.

BIG BELLE: How do you feel, Daddy?

DADDY: Had a real good flake, thanks.
  (chuckling)
You wouldn't read about it, that bus bloke being up the duff.
  (then)
Seen M'daughter Orph yet?

BIG BELLE: No, we haven't, Daddy.

DADDY: Man blinks and look what happens. I don't want to conk out in court. Zizz on the bus.

BIG BELLE: You can zizz out where you want, Daddy.

DADDY: A real good flake, y'know.

BIG BELLE: (nodding) You can flake out where you want, too.

HAMMER: Those zoo keepers tried to kid along the Russian panda with the Chinese panda and nothing came of that pandering.

HORRIE: Here, pussy-pussy...

> *(With utter mischievousness, he pretends to be leading a dog towards DADDY using a bit of wire as a leash. He taunts the old man)*

HORRIE: … play with this.

DADDY: (reacting) You keep that bastard alshay-shun away, you mongrel of a man! I'll sick the police onta ya, Jarvis! Bastard, you.

BIG BELLE: *(*at HORRIE*)* Just step back a mile or two, sport.

HORRIE: Sic'im, Fido!

DADDY: (now spluttering, trying to sit up) Got no flamin' right, Jarvis! Bastard mongrel dog!

BIG BELLE: (stroking his head) Ignore him, love.

DADDY: Sicin' the dog. Public bar, public bar, bastard you!
Bastard alshay-shun!
   (up at her)
Why don't he sook the bastard thing onto those white mongs
brandishing all them billiard cues, eh?

HORRIE: (wickedly) Bow wow! Grrrr!

BIG BELLE: (rising) So help me, Horrie, you...

> *(But she has levered herself up by putting weight on
> DADDY's head. There is a loud crack. DADDY goes
> limp, his head at an awkward angle)*

BIG BELLE: Somebody... help.

HAMMER: Trying to help him would be like trying to wade
left-to-right after Moses crossed right-to-left.

> *(but he does deign to grab hold of DADDY's legs and
> directs as necessary:)*

HAMMER: You ladies on his head. You to the left, me to the
right, and twist. Hold his head down more. Okay. Now.

> *(They give up momentarily in trying to straighten him
> out. Not for the first time they have to look down on
> him)*

HAMMER: What can we do? He was born around here. It's
like water vapour. Given dry conditions, it just offers itself up.
   (*then motions to try straightening him out again*)
Once upon a time, those White cockey holy terrors and our
mob's holy terrors would take it out around the back. No one
gets hurt and it gets the pub floor swept once in a while. Hold
it, let's get him on the grass...
   *(they manage to do so, try unsuccessfully to straighten him
again)*
Uh... hold on. You come down here; me up there.

78

(stopping for another rest)
... But guns are going too far. Going hammer'n'tongs used to be enough, right? Do guns respect the reason why back alleys are there or the only way of getting the pub floor swept once a year? Guns ain't right... Hold it...

(They stand back to gather breath, before HAMMER signals for them to try again)

HAMMER: Try getting that shoulder out of the way. Twist... *harder.* So Endeavour Lane here gets marked on Google Maps for all the telescopic sights being lined up down here. You look along the barrel and... look, you try pulling your end and I'll try mine... and, blow me, if it wasn't after midnight who'd you see? This one. Old Dads here, with his finger in the dyke of what-can't-be-stopped. And what immortal words does he lay down for us all? We get those 'eh? eh?'s. Australia's answer to Nelson Mandela.
(lets the feet drop)
Let's think about this a bit. I might be running out of puff, but wouldn't you think it'd be nice if we could straighten him out just once in his life, ha ha?
(lets everything drop)
Oh, forget it.

(They leave the old man and move away.

HORRIE takes the opportunity of manoeuvring himself towards the bottle of beer again. Just as he is about to commandeer it, DADDY's hand reaches out and grabs it. DADDY wins the tug of war again... only then opens his eyes.)

BIG BELLE: You're going to have to cut this out, Daddy. My ticker's won't stand it.

DADDY: Out to it again, was I, eh?

BIG BELLE: It's just that I don't want anybody to have to smack my bum to get *me* going.

DADDY: Had this real pig of a dream about that mongrel Jarvis. Mongrel of an al-shay-shun of his.

HORRIE: (deliberately impish) I'm Jarvis.

DADDY: (instantly) You started it, bloody Jarvis. You didn't have to throw my boys out!
  (so upset, nearly has another fit)
Don't… wanna… cough…

ORPH: (patting his back) You cough.

HORRIE: Cough off.

ORPH: Go ahead and cough. I've seen them cough and look better for not coming out of it.

> *(DADDY recovers enough. BIG BELLE signs for them to lift him onto the couch, but he goes limp when they try. They give up yet again and leave him be.*
>
> *A long pause, before DADDY sits up suddenly, searches pockets and thankfully finds the ticket he was, and is, looking for. Then lies back comatose again)*

BIG BELLE: Fuck, don't let him go off again!

> *(But nobody now wants to be the first to come forward. The women finally draw apart and sit on the couch looking down at him.)*

ORPH: You can get fooled, though. Some of the major muscles can be stimulated later than you think. You could be putting on some eye liner then suddenly the face twitches. It can really ruin the effect you've been striving for.

(Finally, HAMMER dutifully and wearily gets up to try again)

HAMMER: Be honest now. Let's say it for all the Moree who encouraged him to catch a nonexistent bus to some extinct courthouse in Sydney because they're desperate to get shot of him for a bit?... ready?... so all together now....
  (whether or not any of the others want to join in:)
Get thee to Sydney, Daddy of the Kamilroi! Hie thee unto the court lists. Go hence by departing hince!

> *(He tries to cajole them to join him to try to lift DADDY again, but there are no takers)*

BIG BELLE: (determined mutter) So help me, I'm getting him on that bus if we have to shove him into the luggage compartment.

> *(HAMMER gives up again, dusts hands)*

HAMMER: It's a joy to watch a professional at work. He's been here a... what?... a microdot...

ORPH: (butting in) … a speeding bullet's time...

HAMMER: Right, a speeding bullet's time. And already he's polarised us into sexes.
  (hams it up)
Sexless parts the sexes.

HORRIE: Daddy and his urge tubes!

HAMMER: ('music hall') I say, did you just urge that up?

HORRIE: *(*ditto) I did.

HAMMER: I say, I say, I say. I take it you have hidden talents?

HORRIE: I have hidden urges.

HAMMER: Ha ha.

HORRIE: Thanking you.

HAMMER: No, thanking you.

HORRIE: Oh, I thank you.

HAMMER: No, allow me to thank *you*. Shall we say toodleloo to the nice people and thank the Tourist Bureau for that interesting little old Elder?

TOGETHER: Toodleloo to the nice people and thanks to the Tourist Bureau for the interesting little old Elder.

> *(DADDY sits up all jolly)*

DADDY: Anyone on for a bit of a nibble on the old hard-boiled goog?

> *(and rummages around in pockets to pull out his lunch wrapped in an old newspaper)*

ORPH: Aw. It almost makes you want to forget the ptomaine poisoning before it hits you.

DADDY: M'Orph gives it for the trip, but a bloke never could come at hard-boiled googs. Don't tell her, but.
(offering again)
It's nice'n'fresh. Boilin' gets rid of the chook's shat.

BIG BELLE: Aw.

ORPH: Aw.

82

HAMMER: *(outraged at their gullibility)* I warn you. You fool around with stereotypes and you'll be doing our mob more harm than good. Dummies.
(grabs egg off DADDY; witheringly:)
Hard-boiled, he says. Nice and fresh, he goes.

> *(and, with a flourish, cracks the egg on DADDY's head. It is certainly not hard-boiled but dribbles all over his head. And it is certainly not fresh; they pinch their noses with the smell)*

HAMMER: That's so nice and fresh, it needs a maternity-ward mop and bucket.

DADDY: Bit off, eh?

HAMMER: You may call it off, Daddyo, but I calls it reality.

BIG BELLE: Ain't you enjoying it, though.

HAMMER: Look, ancient and once-noble Kamilroi Dads, I'll try again. To be brutally frank that court case about the riot of Endeavour Lane went on twenty-five years ago. By our count, anyway. It was indeed in Sydney, but that is the only thing you have right is that we haven't added up correctly.

> *(But DADDY merely lies back, closes eyes, after smiling indulgently back at the suggestion.)*

HAMMER: These days they call it Alzheimer's, Daddy, see. You are lying back next to a reconstructed barricade we constructed for one Sunday-morning's look-see and it's so far in the future there's not even blood on the floor of the Imperial's Ladies Lounge anymore. So if you were really waiting for a bus down the lane where the pot shots got potted on the night you think it is, would you really have your lunchy-wunchies wrapped in the Sydney Morning Herald dated with today's date of...?

(He has whipped away the lunch packet to show the newspaper date to DADDY. DADDY looks at it, looks up as though HAMMER isn't all there himself. HAMMER looks more closely at the date line, throws the paper away in disgust.

BIG BELLE gets up retrieves the paper, disgustedly shows the other women)

HAMMER: Are you going to believe that misprinting?

(They stare at him fixedly with thin lips.)

HAMMER: Are you going to believe this bundle of complexes over my bigger bundle of complexes?

DADDY: (haven-safe) We got time to slip down to the Imperial for a quickie?

BIG BELLE: Aw, you'd have to weigh him in as a bit of a doll.

HAMMER: Remember Brer Rabbit and the Tar Baby, I beg you!

DADDY: (about HAMMER) This mug botherin' you?

HAMMER: Did I hear right?

DADDY: You havin' a go at the ladies? Hey, mug, one arm tied behind me back, one arm tied behind me back!

(But he is distracted by the sound over of the braking of a bus on gravel, then revving of the engine)

DADDY: Hey, somebody hoi that bloody driver!

BIG BELLE: *(but energy gone)* Don't, love.
(then thinks about it)

84

I think I *did* hear a bus. You hear a bus?

McINTOSH: I did.

HAMMER: *No bus.*

ORPH: I distinctly heard a bus.

DADDY: (still scrambling about) I got everything?

(Sound of a bus taking off in gravel, doing a wheelie)

DADDY: HEY!

P.A.: 'Announcement, passengers. The express bus to Sydney via the Ned Kelly Bar will be delayed by ten minutes while the driver returns to the Depot to put his teeth in. We remind passengers the destination is Sydney and all should spruce up a bit. Make Moree proud.'

DADDY: Bit of a relief, that.
  (*at BIG BELLE*)
You taking the bus too?
  (*doesn't wait for reply*)
I said to m'Orphie, I said this time no bastard of a cover-up. I'll get right up that judge.

> *(HORRIE has maliciously signalled to CHINA again, going blink-blink. The high beam headlights come to nail DADDY again. The old man struggles to, but can't, 'push' against them as much as he tries to fight against them)*

DADDY: Orright, you young blokes, you've had your fun! Garn home! We got women down here!

> *(Another shot. They all duck, except HORRIE who waves his bat)*

85

HORRIE: Hey, China, fair warning!

(But has to abort that, like the others, he sees DADDY tottering then falling once more, this time as though shot.

Still, they have gotten used to this enough by now that no one moves to him. It is left to HAMMER to approach him casually)

HAMMER: The bodies are beginning to pile up. This is what I wanted us all to look-see… a normal Sunday morning down Endeavour Lane. In Moree, you just wait and it comes to you. Didn't I say that?

(DADDY stirs to a violent coughing attack again. They watch him unable to bring themselves to help)

BIG BELLE: That's it. Coming, Orph?

ORPH: I'd just like to say… well, no, I wouldn't, actually.

(Once more the two women go to move off but, at her first few backing steps before turning to leave, DADDY cunningly rolls groaningly into BIG BELLE's path. She near trips over him yet again)

BIG BELLE: *Shit!*

ORPH: Please be careful.

BIG BELLE: Well, what's he doing down there? I need a drink. Who's got a drink?

McINTOSH: I had some but I drank it all. Boy, did that lay into me too.

BIG BELLE: (still blaming HAMMER) I can't believe my eyes this is going on.

HAMMER: Ah, the eyes.

BIG BELLE: Yeah, eyes. You live another million years, you might develop some on stalks.

HAMMER: Who needs them to see…
   (re DADDY)
that? Seeing is only luffing up.

ORPH: It's not something I'm asked from the slab very often. Don't ask me what.

> *(Almost with relief, they sink back into listening to DADDY'S discomfort. But, again, he surprises them with his hold-on:)*

DADDY: A man gets used to the aches here'n'there.

ORPH: *(hiss to the others)* We still should be straightening him out before he sets hard and won't fit in storage. It's a perennial problem when the business isn't expanding as fast as the rent.
   (gets no offers of help)
Daddy, you'll feel better up on the couch. Let's get him on the couch.

> *(Wearily, BIG BELLE joins in to try again to lift him, but again he goes limp. They give up, renew seats.*
>
> *First one, then the others, watch the circling of an eagle above, until:)*

DADDY: Glad m'boy didn't live to see this day.
Alive'n'kickin', he'd be up the lane there knocking a few of them white larries' heads together.

HAMMER: (really fed up now) Old man, if you want, you can leave your business card with our man China currently available up at the end you're talking about. The thing is, we'll ringbark you; don't you ringbark us.

DADDY: (surprisingly angry) Yain't throwin' us out. We got our rights! What sorta mongrel?

(Another interruption:)

P.A.: 'Yes, Your Honour. Well, I am Thomas Foster, Superintendent to Dr Newton at the Big River Station near Myall Creek. A few weeks after the reported disappearance of the Dangar Kamilroi mob, I was satisfied in my own mind that the large body I saw on the rise above Dangar Station was that of Daddy the black; it was lying on its back, but I could not say how the head was taken off; there was a little flesh on the body. There were several heads with the flesh on them; I could not recognise any of them; there were some males and females lying about; there were several heads of which the fire had not burned the hair; the heads appeared to me to have been taken off. I stopped about twenty minutes at the place; the smell was very offensive and I found it overpowered me...'

(HAMMER launches himself towards the lane's end)

HAMMER: China, blow it outa your ear!

HORRIE: Hey, boss, you know China. Don't even bother getting them in a knot.

HAMMER: They are not in a knot. I can reposition them. Left to right, right to left. I can hoist them. I can bam them, wham them, slam them on the floor, jam them in the door. As a throw-in special I might even be able to throw them over my shoulder like a Continental soldier. But I cannot, repeat cannot, *knot* them.

BIG BELLE: Just don't knot them.

HAMMER: I just admitted I cannot knot them.

88

ORPH: Well, you can actually…

BIG BELLE: All right, don't get them in a twist.

HAMMER: You cannot *get* them in a twist. They are either in a permanent state of twist or a permanent state of untwist. If you try to *get* them to reverse in a lateral way than they permanently *are*, they will just, as in the sing-a-long, zong back as in ouch.

BIG BELLE: You've got nothing to sing-a-long about.

(Strained silence)

DADDY: You blokes getting sarky with each other?

BIG BELLE: Dads, we're all feeling a bit bombed out, that's all. This is the longest Sunday morning since before the whitefellah came over the rise, you know?

DADDY: Why dontcha just shoot off. Don't worry about me.

(They watch in half-amazement while he repositions himself on the old couch, looking very comfy.)

DADDY: That bus'll have to see me or run a bloke over. 'Sides, my Orph'll front up soon.

(It is HORRIE who this time is not going to take the old man's emotional blackmail lying down. He brandishes the bit of wire he used before as a dog on a leash)

HORRIE: Hey, deadhead, is this savage animal going to tear you from limb to limb? Is this an alsatian
   (shakes it)
straining at the leash to get at your scrawny neck? Bow wow. Grrrr, grrrr.

DADDY: Y'keep that bastard mongrel tied up, Jarvis!

HORRIE: Look, shit-for-brains, do I look the publican type? I look like one who would give a shit about banning anyone for colour? Okay, forget I asked that. You could come from a line of purple-people eaters for all I care, as long as you wanted to drink yourself silly on that side of the bar which ain't my side of the bar. So put a pipe in it and scoot.

DADDY: The coppers'll put that bastard of an alshayun down!

> *(HORRIE furiously returns to try again, applauded by HAMMER)*

HORRIE: Look, you shrinkage you…
  (indicates BIG BELLE)
would you believe she's a midwife with those biceps? She uses grappling irons because her wrists are too big for the human body. She does. When she's finished, they give you a war service medal. Would you believe she moonlights sucking out septic tanks?

BIG BELLE: Rave on.

HORRIE: And her...
  (indicates ORPH)
would you believe her own kids have signed a petition to have her cauterised from having any more of them and her lips sealed as a temporary measure?

ORPH: I will ignore that.

HORRIE: And him…
  (indicates HAMMER)
you believe any off-season, he makes a crust scraping fleas off pets?

HAMMER: It's *grooming*, you dope!

DADDY: (meaning them all) M'Orph acquainted with any of youse?

(HORRIE gives up. But it has given a bit of an opening and HAMMER cannot resist taking it)

HAMMER: Daddy, would you believe he likes nothing better than being in the cow shed pulling the bull's sperm out of the dry ice and getting all Voodoo over each batch he hands over, going
Hoolie hoolie hoolie
Me got no fam-ooly
Give em one for me.
  (*and*)
You believe that, Daddy?
  (indicating BIG BELLE)
And would you believe if I told you that all those little-ickle babies of hers are the luckiest babies in all Australia, Daddy, because when she smacks them on the bot, it's the hardest knock they're ever going to get in life?

BIG BELLE: I'll give you the hardest knock you've ever had in your life.

HAMMER: Daddy of the Kamilroi, this is real! If I told you, would you believe then...
  (*indicates ORPH*)
she's *the* undertaker in this town because her boss gets hay fever around dead bodies because they get all dusty out this way? Also, no one makes her clients look better. Ding dong, she's Avon's best customer. By the time she's finished with you, Dads, they send you off with shipboard streamers. It's true. She wasn't Miss Wharfside Send-off for two years in a row for nothing.

(Still gets nothing out of DADDY)

HAMMER: (indicating McINTOSH) Dads, see him? Surely, you'll recognise him. You wouldn't believe if I told you how hard it is to tell him apart from your young Ronald McIntosh.

DADDY: Young Cheeky?

HAMMER: That's the one.

DADDY: Don't know him.

BIG BELLE: Sure you do, Daddy. Young Cheeky. He sat by your son's bedside at the end when nobody else would come near him. Would what they call a good-for-nothing in court do that?

HAMMER: (given boost) Cheeky McIntosh, Pops. Remember how he was the bright star of Moree? Double century for Moree Firsts at the age of 11? The Moree Run Machine? National representative under 18, carrying all of Moree hopes since the age of fifteen?

HORRIE: But gets thrown out of the squad for possession. Comes back with his tail between his legs...?

McINTOSH: (anguish) That was just *holding*! They really lay into you for that down there in Melbourne!

DADDY: (sadly) Young Cheeky, eh? Stubborn little bugger, wouldn't listen.

HAMMER: (seeing progress) Turned out just another failure of one of your boys, right, Dads? But would you believe what they found on his computer, Daddy? None of the usual porn. They found an application for entry into Sydney Uni. Under the form's 'school level reached' Cheeky had put

McINTOSH: (misery) 'Got caught holding and laid into'.

HAMMER: Correct.

McINTOSH: Can I get paid now?

DADDY: Cheeky.

McINTOSH: Yessir, Cheeky.

DADDY: Keen on m'Orph, young Cheeky is.

> *(In a surprise move, he turns hard and knowing eyes on ORPH)*

DADDY: Hello, Orphie. Bout time you come.

> *(ORPH is thrown, doesn't know how to react)*

ORPH: (dully) Hello.

> *(She gets urgent encouragement from HAMMER to take it further:)*

ORPH: Hello.

BIG BELLE: (warning) Here, don't you go making him peg out again.

HAMMER: It might work, you know.

BIG BELLE: It won't.

HAMMER: Say, hypothetically.

DADDY: (mutter) Hypothetically.

> *(HAMMER is encouraged)*

HAMMER: Okay, Dads, say that Horrie... alright the dastardly Jarvis... trots back in here holding hands with an Orphie Robson, and all she's wearing is your boy's jarmie top

93

and she shouts at you come back home you silly old Daddy you, we've been looking all night up here and down Sydney way? What then?

(DADDY remains obstinately mute. As a sort of inducement,

HAMMER motions HORRIE to go off down the lane to look for the old man's daughter. HORRIE very reluctantly does so, while:)

HAMMER: What if he finds her? Nothing? Another black out? Clunk, crash, slam, click, and the old mental iron grill comes crashing down again?
  (*then*)
No, don't go off. Would you believe that?

(still no reply; indeed DADDY now seems to have gone unheeding of everything other than trying to get his shirt off.)

HAMMER: Let me help you with that.

(as HAMMER helps, DADDY mesmerically just doesn't stop at the shirt but starts taking everything else off too, and:)

DADDY: M'Orph's all I got now. Bloody hell, you should've seen that leukemia thing turn my poor kid black as a dingo's cakehole. What a bastard of a thing. Thirteen. That night he went off, his little chest just cracked opened and it started pouring out. It did. He said to me, 'Daddy, can I've a cuppa coffee?' I said, 'Can't it wait for pension day, son?" He said no he didn't think it could, like. Oh, he knew orright. I got him that cuppa coffee, borrowed from Belle. He was bleeding all over the bed from his little chest. It was the coffee that did it. I said, 'Try to hold it in, son.' He said to me, 'No worries, Dad.' Jeez, he was bleeding, eh? From the chest, then the arms. Black as the ace of spades he went... Yeah, young Cheeky was

94

there holdin' his hand, come to think of it. Good boy, that
Cheeky.
(has to stop a painful moment)
So I rushed over and told the Father. I said, 'Father, my boy's
bleeding like Jesus back there…' 'Sorry, the matron gone
home on holiday', Father said, 'and the doctor's still five years
away'.
(finally)
I told you this before?'

> *(DADDY is now left only in his underpants, waits on*
> *HORRIE as to whether he found the daughter, but*
> *HORRIE avoids any eye contact, goes back to join*
> *McINTOSH at the barricade)*

HAMMER: Well?

HORRIE: Well, what?

HAMMER: Look, that go-off, come-back blank-stare's been
done.

HORRIE: So?

HAMMER: *His daughter, man.*

> *(HORRIE can only just shrug. He is trying to hide being*
> *genuinely confused himself. He shapes up at the crease,*
> *motions to CHINA)*

HAMMER: Belay that!

> *(HAMMER looks at HORRIE closely)*

HORRIE: (refusing to talk about it) We going out tomorrow?
You got in the goods from that bull in Scotland?

HAMMER: Don't you go getting weird on me too.

(But DADDY is already motioning to ORPH to show her something... seemingly apropos of nothing... on his bum by lifting his underpants)

DADDY: See what I mean?

ORPH: (looking) You know I've never seen one of those on the living in my life but then I guess how do I know the living would have one of those if I've never seen one?

HAMMER: (near terminally disgusted) Sympathy for some wear'n'tear below the belt doesn't count.

ORPH: (high horse) If you must know, I was looking to see if he had one above the belt.

HAMMER: It's always below the belt.

ORPH: You look.

HAMMER: I don't think so.

DADDY: Hey, where's m'fifty?

BIG BELLE: (at HAMMER) Give it back.

DADDY: *(*not in wallet*)* Anyone seen a fifty kickin' around?

HAMMER: Is this his formal objection we all have been waiting for?

BIG BELLE: I said give it back.

HAMMER: (ignoring her, to DADDY*)* If you feel I might have had something to do with some fifty, feel free to object.

DADDY: What's a man gonna do now? Them courts in Sydney come good with free accommodation?

HAMMER: I demand satisfaction by you objecting.

BIG BELLE: He's not objecting just so you can call it a day and make off with his fifty, sport.

HAMMER: For God's sake, if you're going to make an International Court of the Hague case out of it, I'll lend him a fifty I rescued from the bull ants.

(and shoves it in a pocket of the overnight bag.)

BIG BELLE: You didn't come out from the womb right, you didn't.

HAMMER: I suppose it would be useless to point how my rich Maori uncle-in-law still refuses my allowance. Poor me.

DADDY: *(indicating clothes)* You finished with these, mate?

HAMMER: Oh, stop complaining!

> *(He steps away and, inevitably, trips over something of DADDY's. This time it's his overnight bag.*
>
> *This he angrily grabs hold of and, expecting it to be heavy, heaves on it. It is as light as a feather and this causes him to stumble backwards and to fall heavily and undignified among the barricade rubble)*

HAMMER: God dammit!

> *(and flings off the seeming empty bag)*

DADDY: Hey, watchit!

> *(He struggles to retrieve it. When DADDY picks it up, it is like it is laden with rocks and he struggles with it)*

HORRIE: Look at the old goat now!

BIG BELLE: Daddy love, don't try our patience anymore, okay?

DADDY: (having to drag it back) A man.... ain't… what he used...

HORRIE: Hey, dumbo, the only thing more empty would be your head.

DADDY: Hey, don't go all dippy on a man! Belle, why would a bloke lug along an empty bag?

BIG BELLE: Daddy, just take it from us your bag's empty or nears about. Come round to my place tomorrow and I'll fill it with all the male leftovers I've got hanging around.

DADDY: I'll be in court tomorrow.

BIG BELLE: So's most of the males I got leftovers from. Lucky that's all I got from them.

> *(DADDY realises they might not be friends after all, but only out to ridicule him. He recoils by backing away from them all, dragging his bag after him.*
>
> *HORRIE gets angry at this 'stupid' display again. He snatches the overnight bag… hardly a weight… away.)*

HORRIE: Look!

> *(He roughly unzips the bag, shoves it under DADDY's nose. It is empty.)*

DADDY: Mongrel you, Jarvis, you look...!

> *(DADDY unzips the bag. A few contents spill out as though it was overflowing. He gets down in his hands and knees to retrieve them and secure the case again.)'*

HAMMER: (looking) Condoms?

DADDY: Never trust them Sydney sorts. Passed on down generations, that bit of advice.

HORRIE: (exploding) Look, you!

> (and grabs bag back, hoists it high with one little finger, throws it down.)

DADDY: No, look!

> (and only just manages to drag it back under his protection)

HORRIE: Don't tell me to look, muxcronk! You look!

> (and hoists it from DADDY with one little finger again. He does an aeroplane spin with it. In the middle of this, the handle breaks and the rest of the bag flies off to land on DADDY and knocks him down. He lies there, eyes wide open and unblinking, under the weight of it.
>
> They gather around him, getting good at doing so by now.)

HAMMER: What do you think the percentage of that happening again would be?

BIG BELLE: Don't even bother to think about it.

> (But none of them have any energy to try to help him anymore. Finally HAMMER bends over him to lift one of his eyelids and holds it open for ORPH)

HAMMER: See if you can keep this open.
  (then into DADDY's ear)
One, two, one two three.... anything eyes-wise?

ORPH: (shaking head) Like underneath an integrated circuit you have to occasionally search the wrists for and not finding a pulse and asking yourself what's the point of having a pace maker?

HAMMER: One, two, one two three...

ORPH: Yes! Stop the injections!

HAMMER: (genuinely interested) Did I say injections?
   (*then*)
Never mind. That's a response noted in one eye. Now, see if you can hold both open.
   (*she manages to do so. He carries on speaking in DADDY's ear*)
Daddy of the Kamilroi, you are looking upwards Kamilroi-wise. You mustn't think that this overnight bag was doing anything personal. It's only because you're still flat out on your back in the Ned Kelly bar with a lump on your head the size of a cue ball, which would be right since a cue ball probably caused it, or you haven't yet registered that you've just been clobbered while coming between a lot of drunks rioting and another lot of drunks rioting down here by the bull ants of Endeavour Lane. The thing is, wherever you go, there's some overnight bag flying around.
   (*pauses*)
Dads, it comes down to a thing called grief. Living on the margins, you might have heard of it. In cows' cases, it's thought to open the bowels.
   (*to ORPH*)
Anything?

ORPH: Nothing that I'd tip him off a slab for.

HAMMER: (carries on) See, Daddy, what you need is a quick jab of reality.
   (*calls up the lane*)
Trot along with that Moree Plains canvas, China!

(waits, has to try again)
The Moree Plains. Moree Plains!
(while waiting; back to DADDY)
Replete, if you'll look closely, with not one Kamilroi in sight
but oodles of tourist traps. Now, why do you think there is no
Kamilroi only a lot of tourists, Daddy…?

> *(But still no backdrop. He strides angrily off. The
> others wait, eyes upwards towards where the flies would
> be back in the theatre.*
>
> *HAMMER returns)*

HAMMER: (shivers) Deserted, like…

BIG BELLE: Well, what are you? No hands?

HAMMER: Usually, you'd expect it to just drop from the
sky…

BIG BELLE: Shit'n'sugar, everybody's gone bloody useless…

> *(She strides off herself to get the backdrop. Returns
> almost immediately and, like the others before her, sits
> down glumly without volunteering a word.*
>
> *An unattached scene cloth gets thrown in from the lane,
> virtually almost falling out of the sky. It lands on and
> buries DADDY. Still, they can only stare down at him.)*

BIG BELLE: It's like beating a beach ball over the head with a
mallet.

> *(They finally help each other get it off DADDY. He
> remains pinned by the overnight bag, but at least has got
> a bit of his old self back again)*

DADDY: Old footy injury... can't lift like I usedta.

101

HAMMER: (to others) You win. I'm Pontius Pilate, where's the soap?

(Nobody is volunteering to take over. The void is filled, anyway, with a burst of:)

P.A.: 'Yes, Your Honour. Well, I remain Thomas Foster, Superintendent to Dr Newton at the Big River Station near Myall Creek. The stockmen were said to have chased the Kamilroi about the area, cutting off their heads like chickens and throwing the bodies off to one side over the fence rails, which were saturated with blood to such an extent that cattle could only be driven there with the greatest difficulty because of the latent smell...'

HAMMER: (shouting) I'm going to the chasing and it'll be after you, China!

(But instead there is another immediate P.A. burst:)

P.A.: 'On the first count of murder of... *(sound emphasis)* ... ORPHIE ROBSON, DAUGHTER OF DADDY ROBSON... using sound capital letters without shouting in the court, how do you find the first defendant?' Guilty as charged? Not guilty as not charged? On the second count of murder of the Aboriginal elder known as... *(emphasis)*... DADDY ROBSON, FATHER OF ORPHIE ROBSON... again using sound capital letters and without shouting in the court, how do you find the first defendant, not guilty as not charged or guilty as charged...?'

BIG BELLE: *What names were they*?!

ORPH: *Ssh*!

BIG BELLE: (fightingly) Ssh what?

ORPH: *Do you hear the fallen squeaking?*

(and throws herself down upon the ground with such urgency that the others instinctively follow.

Immediately there rings out a whole volley of rifle shots and shotgun blasts... it is a shocking sound effect.

DADDY is actually the first to recover from the shock. He rolls out from under the overnight bag)

DADDY: ORPH?!

(The volley is then followed by a burst of headlights that pick DADDY out. Accompanying it is shouted racial abuse from down the lane.)

DADDY: (shout back) *What're you done to m'Orphie?!*

(He stands holding his hands out against what seems to be coming on. When nothing immediately eventuates, he turns on HAMMER and the others)

DADDY: (growl, but in shock) What've you mob done to m'Orphie?

(This time he really falls to his knees, rocking with grief, even more momentarily beyond their help. They try comfort from afar)

BIG BELLE: We've only got a sick bugger called China up the lane fooling around, Daddy.

HAMMER: (really interested) Do you think he gets that?

ORPH: What she means is ours in the nature of things while the pulse's doing its rounds, Daddy. It's not the same as hay shining.

HAMMER: She is groping for the words 'It's only our better nature', Daddy.

BIG BELLE: What this greedy pig is trying to say is that we can't be what you want us to be, not on Sunday mornings, Daddy.

HAMMER: What she is trying to say is, our real faces are behind our masks because we're on the verge of where everything shitty happened, Dads.
  (*afterthought*)
I tell you what we can do, though. We can all shout with you. That help?

> *(He motions for unanimity of action and gets it grudgingly for shouting:)*

ALL: ORPHIE?!

> *(Now DADDY definitely knows there is something terribly wrong)*

DADDY: YOU BUGGERS!

> *(He leaps up with surprising violence – only in his underpants -- and swings his overnight bag around to keep them at bay.*
>
> *When they stand back to give him wide berth, he makes a break for it.*
>
> *Only McINTOSH is quick enough to reach him. He makes a grab for DADDY, catches only the band of his shorts.*
>
> *DADDY's surprising rage in tugging back has the underpants torn right off him.*
>
> *The old man dashes off nude, crying out primordially)*

BIG BELLE: (blaming HAMMER of course) Now what've you done?

HAMMER: Gut me. Go the draw-and-quarter.

> *(McINTOSH holds up DADDY's underpants by two fingers before discarding them)*

McINTOSH: What'll I do with these? Yerk.

> *(Since no one volunteers to take them, he puts them rather neatly on the barricade like they were a flag.*
>
> *A long pause. They expect to hear something bad off, but nothing comes. They feel empty suddenly that DADDY isn't there)*

HAMMER: At least he got a real good mention.

ORPH: (nodding) It's always best to see if the Obituaries have gone out before tearing off the wrappers.

HAMMER: ('dusting off hands') So, I think that was worth it, don't you? A good look-see's better out than in, or what?
    (and)
Horrie, dyou think China can give us a bit of light?

> *(HORRIE obliges by signalling down lane. The headlight beams come on again.*
>
> *They don't focus where HAMMER quite wants them, and, to the others' impatience, fusses to get them just right)*

HORRIE: Dip, China!

> *(When they do so, it only requires a bit of signalled adjustment to get the headlight to pick out DADDY's clothes against the barricade as HAMMER wants. Now*

105

HAMMER, the writer/director back in charge of the sight-seeing workshop again, stands over the spotlight area and:)

HAMMER: Well, hello Daddy!

BIG BELLE: Don't you dare.

HAMMER: (mock plea) I'm begging you.

BIG BELLE: Yeah, and who's begging?

HAMMER: An ordinary man.

BIG BELLE: Yeah, how ordinary?

HAMMER: A fairly ordinary man.

BIG BELLE: Who?

HAMMER: A very ordinary man. A VIP of an ordinary man.

BIG BELLE: (giving in) I'm watching you, that's all, sport.

(So encouraged, HAMMER rounds on the spotlit clothes. He fumbles in his pocket for the right piece of paper)

HAMMER: I have just the thing for now.
  (*reads, recites*)
The supercilious silliness
Of this poor wingless bird
Is cosmically comic
And stellarly absurd.

(He places his foot in the light and on the clothes)

HAMMER: To conclude, mes enfants. Daddy. Right here.
I'm going to speculate. He came by dreaming he'd found this

106

sacred cave and in there were whole mob of ancestral Kamilroi
Daddies sitting dreaming, and their sacred blood was the great
oozing in the sacred sand soak that made all the rivers run.
And because all their eyes were closed, Daddy knew they were
dreaming, but more especially, they were dreaming of him.
And he knew that if any one of his ancestors woke up and
stopped dreaming about him, then he, Daddy, *would no longer
be.*
   (and)
So, now we've done the veni-vidi-vice bit, I suggest we…

   (But he is instantly interrupted with another:)

P.A.: 'Announcement for all passengers on the flooded side of
the terminus. Please stand by for when the bus from some place
called Goondiwindi passes through, stopping at all towns to
Newcastle going the wrong way, with connections to Sydney if
it can stop to get its brakes repaired. Passengers are advised to
get ready for the leap; the driver is due in court and is running
late.'

   *(After it fades, HAMMER goes to start up his rhetoric
   again, but is interrupted once more by:)*

P.A.: 'Repeating that the train or bus from some place called
Goondiwindi for Newcastle connecting with Sydney is about to
arrive at platform two in bus stand number four. Stand back on
platform four for the rush from bus stand number two…'

BIG BELLE: That's not China!

ORPH: *Where are we anyway?*

HAMMER: (trying to calm them) We trust each other, don't
we?

ORPH: My God, we're being *slabbed*!

107

HAMMER: No, no. As I was saying, before being rudely interrupted, hasn't…

(indicates DADDY's spotlit clothes)

that Daddy given us a taste of our own Daddy and made it all worthwhile?

> *(He scrambles notes from his pocket, willy-nilly distributes one to each of the others)*

HAMMER: Don't just read these. Remember it's Sunday morning and slow seepage time. *Spread* them around in your minds!

> *(He drops down to sit in a bad imitation of DADDY, with his back against the barricade)*

HAMMER: Here… look, see… I'm *our* Daddy. I'm our work-in-progress. I'm done for! I'm dead beat! You've got me! Finish me off!
(to ORPH)
You first, the ghost of little Orphie. Do me down! Beat me up!

McINTOSH: Lay into him!

> *(ORPH, as do the others, has no trouble picking up on what he means. It is the look-see they were there for, need hardly consult any character notes. They are excited.*
>
> *For ORPH's part, she acts mightily pregnant)*

ORPH: My Daddy!

> *(As soon as she waddles near, HAMMER-AS-DADDY hunches over in pain, holding his own belly. When she scratches her navel, he scratches his navel. When she hoists up an imaginary pregnancy girdle, he hoists up an imaginary pregnancy girdle. When she waddles up and*

108

down in front of him, he wriggles accordingly)

HAMMER-AS-DADDY: (awfully miserably) *What is it?*

ORPH: Three months, Daddy. It just didn't like that bullet in its head. I mean, like, who could blame it?

> *(She steps away to let BIG BELLE through, as HAMMER furtively signals HORRIE to take over:)*

HORRIE: Now the matronly secret love shudder shudder... what a dragon!

> *(BIG BELLE comes up coquettishly to DADDY, and makes clumsy attempts at being flirtatious, affectionate)*

BIG BELLE: (as though to a baby's face) Isn't he just *terrible*?

> *(and punches and pinches DADDY painfully on the arm)*

HAMMER-AS-DADDY: Eh?

BIG BELLE: (again) Isn't he just *terrible*?

> *(She gives him another pinch and a punch which hurts equally)*

HAMMER-AS-DADDY: Eh!

BIG BELLE: Isn't he just *terrible*?

> *(She gives him another pinch and a punch with a coquettish giggle)*

HAMMER-AS-DADDY: I'll clock you one!

> *(BIG BELLE withdraws flinging her piece of paper away)*

HORRIE has to nudge McINTOSH that it's his turn as a local young Aboriginal like himself – Cheeky McIntosh:)

HORRIE: (introducing) Cheeky McIntosh, once the town's great black hope let-down.

(McINTOSH comes near HAMMER-AS-DADDY, and gets:)

HAMMER-AS-DADDY: Don't let 'em put their boots into you, Cheeky. You being a no-hoper's none of your blame.

McINTOSH: Tha'so?

HAMMER-AS-DADDY: Don't let 'em get on your willy. It's not all your blame you'll end up on a line of sight.

McINTOSH: Tha'so?

HAMMER-AS-DADDY: Get off m'Orphie, you cheeky b. You're to blame!

(McINTOSH pretends he still can't hear a thing, tickles HAMMER-AS-DADDY as he might a child)

McINTOSH: Is the funny old man spouting? What's the funny old man spoutin'? Is the old dudnuts spoutin'?...

(He continues this nastily, until he gets bored and goes back to climb back on the barricade.

HORRIE takes his place, introducing himself)

HORRIE: And now Al Grasby, the once-upon-a-time Minister of Immigration.
  (mock surprise)
Oo, that's me.
  (he comes forward to torment DADDY too)

Hey, my man, did someone tell me as a government we've achieved so much that I can throw an Abo like you out of his own country?

HAMMER-AS-DADDY: No.

HORRIE-AS-MINISTER: The thing to know it definitely wasn't a race riot, Robbo. It wasn't a murder just a loss of a good lad. The main thing is I'm not leaving here until I know where I've thrown you out from. It wasn't jail. That would be back *in,* ha ha. I know, it must have been out of the back of a paddy wagon, otherwise why do we have paddy wagons? That's it. I throw you out the back of a paddy wagon, Robbo?

HAMMER-AS-DADDY: No, you didn't. A bloke went flying when you turned a corner.

HORRIE-AS-MINISTER: (great laugh) That's the leg-up we want!

> *(At his turn, HAMMER throws off 'mantle' of being DADDY, leaps up and, using them as a focal point spotlit, dances around DADDY's heap of clothing:)*

HAMMER:
All Nature werest o'erpotted o' drop-in turf,
Th'dogs didst railments and g-nashings at th'Masters;
Th'Masters didst derailments o'er th'Mistresses;
Th'Mistresses didst g-nashingments o'er th'Dogs;
Surf Sanderson deceased ponst 's Board.

HORRIE: (the chorus)
The publicans went mad and lashed out free grog;
Only a-man-earned-a-hard-thirst with each glog-glog-glog!

HAMMER: Spot on! And so, who here will do something right about these earthly relics of the last of the Kamilrois?

BIG BELLE: Who's going to clean up this damn mess, you mean.

HAMMER: The large lady is right! Take the shirt!

BIG BELLE: Shove it.

HAMMER: No, no! This is your allotted! We all have to…

(BIG BELLE grabs up DADDY's shirt impulsively. She gags when she sees how her hands are affected by it)

BIG BELLE: *Blood*!

(ORPH screams)

HAMMER: Another cheap trick!

(BIG BELLE, ORPH and, belatedly McINTOSH… only because he thinks he ought to follow… storm off.

HAMMER: (after them) It's not blood! If it is, it just need a bit of time to evaporate, that's all!

(He turns to pick up the shirt and the trousers. Immediately his hands are covered with blood too. He goes to wipe it off on his own trousers. The way it smudges makes no doubt about it being real blood.

HAMMER: Wait up!

(He hurries out after them.

This leaves HORRIE alone at the barricade. He is not perturbed, takes up guard at the crease, beckons out for CHINA, shouts:)

HORRIE: See how lucky you can get, China!

(He gets a sound of a fizzing ball, which he elegantly lets through to the keeper.

Now finds himself alone, but is comfortable with this. Steps forward)

HORRIE: Okay… See, once upon a time in a far-off Aboriginal land there was a great tribe called the Kamilroi, led by the mighty warrior named Daddy. We are talking 37,000 years before even Buddha, Mohammed and Christ, and when those three came along they came across a young Kamilroi girl fishing in the most crystal-clear muddy-water billabong you'd ever see, and they said they'd come to visit the great Daddy of the Kamilroi. 'Which one', she asked, 'Daddy 1 or Daddy 2 or Daddy 3 or Daddy 4 or Daddy 5 or Daddy 6 or Daddy 7 or Daddy 8?'. They said, 'We want the Daddy said to be so wise he has hair on his chest that's never been tweaked'. 'Oh well', the girl, answered, 'that could be Daddy 1 or Daddy 1.1 or Daddy 1.2 or Daddy 1.3 or Daddy 1.4 or Daddy 1.5… and by the way if you've got something else to do, the girl said, I'd do it if I were you, because there's still 36,932 years of Daddies to go before you ever even get to sit on a bull-ant's nest down Endeavour Lane way. Well, as I was saying, you might be looking for Daddy 1.5 or Daddy 1.6 or Daddy 1.7 or Daddy 1.8… going all the way up to Daddy 1.132 and then the Daddies start again at Daddy 1.1a and Daddy 1.2b and Daddy 1.2c and Daddy 1.2d and so forth right up to Daddy 1.2z, and then starting again at Daddy 1.3 and then Daddy 1.3a, Daddy 1.3b and so on and so forth until we get to Daddy 2, and then there's Daddy 2.1 and Daddy 2.2 and Daddy 2.3 and so on until we get all the way up to Daddy 2.1a and Daddy 2.1b and Daddy 2.1c and so on. By the time you get to Daddy 6 and Daddy 6.1 and 6.1a n'whatnot, that's when the cold came and the deserts came and the big trees disappeared. So they tell me; I am too young to argue the toss there. Anyway, I could take you up to Daddy 7.9z and then to Daddy 8, but after the school went and I had to leave, eight's as far as I can count'.

(HORRIE throws his 'bat' over his shoulder, and picks

113

up the 'wicket' piece of cardboard HAMMER
maintained the schoolkids were using as a wicket a week
after the riot. Goes to wander off, then turns to confront
the audience directly again:)

HORRIE: Spooky? Here's something more spooky than that.
You see this cardboard box? It ain't the cardboard box that the
schoolkids were using as a wicket later on... like, not really.
It's
    (turns it around to show blood-splatter stains)
where they should've taken young Cheeky's blood sample
from.

(He goes but stops just before leaving)

HORRIE: What's even more spooky is that a bright kid like
that one with Buddha, Mohammed and Christ had to leave
school.

(He departs)

(End)